BANKING
RISK MANAGEMENT
IN A GLOBALIZING
ECONOMY

BANKING
RISK MANAGEMENT
IN A GLOBALIZING
ECONOMY

Panos Angelopoulos and
Panos Mourdoukoutas

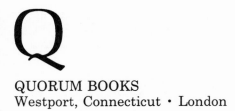

QUORUM BOOKS
Westport, Connecticut · London

Library of Congress Cataloging-in-Publication Data

Angelopoulos, Panos.
  Banking risk management in a globalizing economy / Panos Angelopoulos and Panos Mourdoukoutas.
    p.   cm.
  Includes bibliographical references and index.
  ISBN 1–56720–340–X (alk. paper)
  1. Bank management.   2. Risk management.   I. Mourdoukoutas, Panos.   II. Title.
HG1615.A56   2001
332.1′068′1—dc21   00–062531

British Library Cataloguing in Publication Data is available.

Library of Congress Catalog Card Number: 00–062531
ISBN: 1–56720–340–X

First published in 2001

Quorum Books, 88 Post Road West, Westport, CT 06881
An imprint of Greenwood Publishing Group, Inc.
www.quorumbooks.com

Printed in the United States of America

The paper used in this book complies with the
Permanent Paper Standard issued by the National
Information Standards Organization (Z39.48–1984).

10 9 8 7 6 5 4 3 2 1

To our parents
Christos, Panagiota, Georgios, and Anastasia

Contents

Figures and Tables   ix

1 Introduction: From Financial Intermediation
   to Risk Management   1

2 Banking Risk Management: An Overview   11

3 Evolution of Banking Risk Management   51

4 Risk Management Methods: Financial Derivatives   73

5 Credit Risk Management   97

6 Interest Rate Risk Management   109

7 Foreign Exchange Risk Management   135

8 Conclusion   155

   References   163

   Index   169

Figures and Tables

FIGURES

1.1 Financial Derivatives Value (1988–1998)   7

2.1 Risk versus Return: Riskier Assets Command
Higher Return   41

2.2 Portfolio Diversification and Volatility   42

2.3 Five-Year Treasury Note Daily-Yield Distribution   44

3.1 Gosou Sendan Houshiki   57

3.2 Asset Accumulation and Financial Intermediation
in Japan and the United States (1954–1988)   59

3.3 The Disbanding of Gosou Sendan Houshiki   68

4.1 Classification of Options Contracts   79

4.2 Time Value of an Option's Contract   86

6.1 Buyer and Seller Losses in a Simple FRA   115

6.2 Interest Rate Cap   123

6.3 Interest Rate Floor   125

6.4 Interest Rate Collar   126

6.5 The Olympic Bank and Aegean Credit Interest
Rate Swap   129

6.6 The Olympic Bank and Aegean Credit Interest Rate
Receipts and Payments in a Dealer Swap   131

7.1 Hedging a Short Position with FX Forward Contracts   139

7.2 Currency Swap between Banks A and B   153

TABLES

2.1 Banking Risks   16

2.2 Single and Aggregate Risk Measures   23

2.3 Maturity Ladder for a Representative Bank   25

2.4 Simple and Modified Duration Calculations   32

2.5 Alternative Simple and Modified Duration Calculations   32

2.6 Zero-Coupon Bond, Simple and Modified Duration   33

2.7 Cumulative Gap   36

2.8 Foreign Exchange Price Fluctuations, Net Positions,
and Income Changes   38

2.9 Application of Foreign Exchange Price Fluctuations,
Net FX Positions, and Income Changes   40

3.1 Evolution of Banking Risks in the Twentieth Century   53

4.1 Global Positions in OTC Derivative Markets by Type
of Risk Instrument as of June 1998   74

4.2 Selective Future Contract Margins as of May 13, 1999   77

4.3 S&P Market Value and Option Premiums   84

5.1 Scoring and Asset Classification   101

6.1 Interest Rate Gaps, Interest Rate Fluctuations,
and Revenue Changes   111

6.2 Interest Rate Fluctuations and Selective On-Balance
Sheet Risk Management   112

6.3 Interest Rate Fluctuations and Selective Off-Balance
Sheet Risk Management   113

6.4 Global Positions in OTC Interest Rate Derivatives
as of June 1998   114

6.5 Selective Interest Rate Futures   117

6.6 Selective U.S. Treasury Futures Options   121

6.7 Interest-Rate Risk Management through Receiver's and Payer's Swaption 122

6.8 Interest Rate Cap: An Application 124

7.1 Global Positions in OTC Foreign Exchange Derivative Contracts as of June 1998 137

7.2 Selective FX Futures 145

7.3 Margin Account and the Marking-to-Market (Buyer–Long Position) 146

7.4 Margin Account and the Marking-to-Market (Seller–Short Position) 147

7.5 Profits and Losses for the Straddle Holder 150

7.6 Receipts and Payments in a Foreign Currency Swap 154

Introduction: From Financial Intermediation to Risk Management

1

> Obviously banks make money by taking risks and lose money by not managing risks effectively. To produce superior shareholder returns in current markets, banks must take on higher levels of risk than in the past.
>
> Edward E. Furash (1994, 34)

> We bankers must develop cultures that foster and reward the management of risk. We must continually update our risk-management policies to ensure that they reflect changing industry dynamics.
>
> Marshall N. Carter (1995, 26)

At a mouse click, one can surf the Net and shop for the best Certificate of Deposit (CD) rates. At another click, one can shop for the best mortgage rates. At a third click, one can buy stocks, bonds, mutual funds, and insurance. Sometimes, the seller of CDs, mortgages, stocks, mutual funds, and insurance is a bank around the corner. At other times, the seller is a financial service or an investment securities company somewhere around the country, or around the globe.

New technology, government deregulation, and globalization are changing the financial service industry, and the banking industry in particular, expanding both opportunities and risks. Banking is no longer confined to traditional financial intermediation catered to domestic and local depositor and borrower in a highly regulated low-risk environment. Banking extends to a broad range of financial products previously offered by other segments of the financial service industry catered to the global individual and institutional investor. At the same time, banking is facing increasing competition from other segments of the financial service industry and volatile money and capital markets. Banking is turning into a dynamic and active risk management process of assets and liabilities in a low-regulated high-risk environment.

An inquiry into banking risks and their management in a globalizing economy, this book has a dual objective. First, to take a close look at the transformation of the banking industry from passive financial intermediation to active asset–liability risk management process, and at the sources of traditional and nontraditional banking risks, their measurement, monitoring, and control. Second, to review the conventional, "on-balance sheet," and modern, "off-balance sheet," risk management methods for controlling banking risks with emphasis on the application of financial derivatives to control three core banking risks: credit risk, interest rate risk, and foreign exchange risk.

For the four decades that followed the end of the Great Depression, multinationalization, the division of the world market into separate national and local markets, information inefficiencies, active government intervention and long-term relations created a sanctuary, a low-risk environment for many of the world's large multinational corporations. Tariffs and quotas limited competition across national markets while government regulation limited competition and price fluctuations in local markets. Information inefficiencies and the lack of knowledge of the peculiarities and specificity of certain industries discouraged market entry. A fixed foreign exchange and interest rate regime limited foreign exchange rate and interest rate fluctuations and contained them to one country or region only. Long-term relations between manufacturers, suppliers, and bankers on the one side, and manufacturers, distributors, and retailers on the other, further reduced price fluctuations and market risks.[1]

Multinationalization, information inefficiencies, government regulation, and long-term business relations were extended to the financier of multinational corporations and the banking industry, which also enjoyed its own sanctuary. Multinationalization, for instance, protected banks from foreign competition. Government regulation, geographical barriers, close day-to-day supervision, and interest rate controls limited competition within the industry. Information inefficiencies and licensing requirements protected banks from competition from other segments of the financial industry, namely the securities and insurance industries. Long-term relations further limited banking to a selected group of corporate clients, especially in the Asian countries and most notably Japan, where banks were at the center of *keiretsu* relations, organizing loan consortia on behalf of their clients. Loans were extended at fixed rates for a fixed term and constituted only one of the many relations between lenders and borrowers. "Lending by banks has been at fixed rates for fixed terms, with only moderate discrimination between the best and the clearly less than best borrowers. The decision to be made is whether to make the loan or not. The sense of the price of the loan is complicated by the fact that the loan is normally only one of the number of relationships between the lender and the borrower" (Mayer 1999).

Banking was reduced to a routine process, the monitoring of money flows in and out of the bank coffers, and the mastering of relations with corporate clients. The banking industry as a whole could grow and prosper through financial intermediation, that is, by amassing deposits and dispensing loans, earning seigniorage income, especially in the 1950s and the 1960s, when the industry rode on three favorable trends. First, robust economic growth and disposable income provided for both a steady supply of deposits and a steady demand for loans. Second, a normal yield curve allowed banks to borrow low at the short end and lend high at the long end. Third, rising asset values, often placed as loan collateral, provided a hedge against borrowers' failure to repay their loans, government regulators, and central bankers.

At the core of this "relationship banking" was the bank branch. Staffed with professional accountants, credit analysts, and customer relations experts, the branch performed a dual function. First, it closely monitored money flows in and out of the bank coffers and intuitively managed liquidity risk.[2] Second, it collected loan requests, devised lending application procedures, analyzed customers' financial history and personality, and intuitively assessed the probability of loan defaults. "Defaults cannot be entirely avoided. Yet loan charge-off can be reduced by the systematic application and review of lending procedures. Once a credit request is obtained, credit department personnel should analyze the borrower's financial history and character in detail. This analysis should reveal strengths and weaknesses in past performance and indicate the likelihood of timely payment" (Koch 1988, 138).

Since the mid-1970s, globalization, the increasing integration and interdependence of world markets, government deregulation, and the spread of information technology that supports and reenforces it have created an entirely new world for large multinational corporations and the banking industry. On the one side, globalization, deregulation, and the spread of information technology have been a source of opportunity for both multinational corporations and banks. Globalization, for instance, expanded overseas opportunities in both mature and emerging economies. Government deregulation expanded opportunities in domestic and local markets, while the spread of new technologies lowered transaction costs, and contributed to the development of new products and product delivery systems.

On the other side, globalization has eliminated market sanctuaries, compounding risks and uncertainties, especially financial risks. The lifting of government regulation, for instance, has intensified both international and domestic competition, causing wild resource and commodity price fluctuations. The lifting of trade protectionism and the intensification of cross-border competition raised the risks for banks' corporate clients, especially those with a large exposure to the emerging markets of the former communist countries; and the liberalization of foreign exchange and domestic money markets has introduced two additional risks, the foreign exchange and the interest rate risk. The liberalization of foreign exchange and domestic money markets has further increased interdependence among world markets. Like a snow avalanche that gains momentum, economic instability in one region quickly spreads in other regions, magnifying economic and financial risks. "The call to reality came with deregulation and globalization. Deregulation forced financial institutions to pay more attention to the financial markets. Increased trade forced firms to recognize the truly global nature of competition. As a result, corporations cannot afford to ignore financial risks any more" (Jorion 1997, 7).

For the banking industry, government deregulation has allowed banks to diversify their operations by expanding to new geographical territories both in the domestic and global market, and provide products and services previously offered by the security and insurance industries or other segments of the financial service industry. The spread of information technology has lowered the cost of banking services: ATM machines are less expensive and more convenient than traditional branches, telephone banking is less expensive and more convenient than ATM machines, and internet banking is even less expensive and more convenient than telephone banking.

Government deregulation and new technology have intensified competition within the banking industry and between the banking industry and the other segments of the financial service industry, which has drawn the outcry of bank executives. "We're being replaced by Wall Street firms that scrutinize almost anything. These competitors are taking loans out our back door faster than we can bring them in the first door. . . . The banking industry isn't just dwindling—it's dying! We won't be around in another five years unless we face reality and radically change how we treat—and what we offer—our customers" (Crutchfield 1994, 52).

Government deregulation and new technology have severed the one-to-one relationship between banks and their clients, fostering competition and price wars.

The traditional relationship between a bank and its customer had been a one-to-one link, with the bank and the consumer meeting across a table to negotiate a loan or some other deal. But in the new structure, the innovative finance house put itself between the bank and its customer, suggesting ideas to the customer, and expecting the banks to compete on price and quality to provide whatever financial instruments the customer wished. This new marketing structure thus accelerated the introduction of innovations, and at the same time forced more competitive pricing. (OECD 1987, 59)

Compounding the problem of increasing competition and price wars, interest rate and foreign currency liberalization have further introduced two new risks, the interest rate and the foreign currency or foreign exchange risk. Banks with interest rate–sensitive liabilities, for instance, experience a rise in their interest expense when interest rates rise, while banks with interest sensitive assets experience a loss in interest income when interest rates fall. Banks with foreign currency denominated earnings will experience an earnings shortfall should the domestic currency appreciate. Banks with foreign currency denominated assets will experience a decline in the value of these assets, should the domestic currency appreciate against the foreign currency.

Banking is gradually being transformed from a routine personal financial intermediation process to an active impersonal risk management process, from "relationship" banking to "commodity" banking. The banking industry as a whole can no longer grow and prosper through seigniorage income alone, especially in periods of slow economic growth and asset deflation. It must find new sources of income in the other segments of the financial service industry assuming higher risks. "Banks seeking to keep the deposits of customers unhappy with current yields on CDs and earn fees in the process have turned to investment products, but now they must also be prepared for risk" ("Managing Risk" 1994, 86–92). But even banks which have stayed with traditional lending are now assuming higher risks for two reasons. First, fixed rate and fixed term loans and investments have been replaced by floating rate and variable term loans and investments. Second, top quality borrowers have fled to alternative sources of financing, leaving banks with low quality/high risk borrowers. "Business and consumer lending, once stable markets for commercial banks, have become significantly riskier as top-quality credits have fled banking for securitization or the securities markets" (Furash 1994, 34).

Accommodating the transformation of the banking industry are three major developments: First, the revival and extension of risk measurement methods such as Maculay's Duration Analysis, a measurement of the average time it takes for a financial asset to complete its stream of coupon payments; Markowitz's portfolio selection model; and Sharpe's, Lintner's, and Black's Capital Asset Pricing Model, measurements of investment risk; and Value at Risk (VAR), a measurement of market risk. Second, the development of both hardware and software technologies for monitoring financial risk exposure. Third, financial reengineering, the development of financial derivative products, such as Forward Rate Agreements (FRAs), Futures, Options, and Swaps.

Deriving their value from an underlying interest, an equity index, a debt instrument, a currency, and so on, financial derivatives allow financial institutions and investors in general to hedge their balance sheet against financial risks:

- To hedge their balance sheet against short-term interest rate fluctuations, banks can enter Forward Rate Agreements (FRAs), interest rate futures, and interest rate futures options contracts.
- To hedge their balance sheet against medium term interest rate fluctuations they can enter interest rate cap, floor, collar, and swaption agreements.
- To hedge their positions against long-term interest and foreign exchange fluctuations, banks can enter interest rate and foreign currency swap contracts.

One of the major advantages of financial derivatives is that they can be incorporated into a bank's risk management strategy. Financial derivatives provide banks with protection against risks and improve their financial performance by shifting risks to third parties. "With a solid grounding in the basics of derivatives, bankers can appreciate the potential of these instruments to manage a host of risks and to increase profitability through improved performance" (Casserley and Wilson 1994, 42).

Figure 1.1
Financial Derivatives Value (1988–1998)

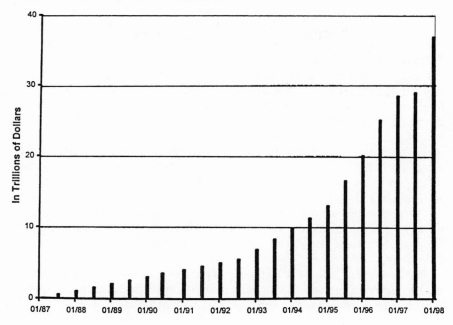

Source: U.S. Comptroller of the Currency, *Quarter Derivative Fact Sheet.*

Financial derivatives also provide protection against financial risks to the world's major corporations.

Southern Company is exposed to market risks in both its trading and non-trading operations. The non-trading operations are exposed to market risks, including changes in interest rates, currency exchange rates, and certain commodity prices. To mitigate changes in cash flows attributable to these exposures, the company has entered into various derivative financial instruments. (Southern Company Annual Report 1997, 28)

The company transacts in foreign currencies, primarily European, and may be exposed to financial and market risk resulting from fluctuations in foreign currency exchange risks, particularly the British pound sterling. The volatility of the pound and other currencies will be monitored in the coming years and the company may utilize hedging programs, currency forward contracts, currency options and/or other derivative financial instruments commonly used to reduce financial market risks. (MTI Technologies Annual Report 1999)

The growing use of financial derivatives by both banks and their corporate clients has created its own fast growing industry, especially in the late 1980s. According to the U.S. Comptroller of the Currency *Quarter Derivative Fact Sheet*, the value of financial derivatives held by U.S. banks reached $38 trillion in the second quarter of 1998 (see Figure 1.1). This staggering figure consists of $10 trillion in futures and forwards contracts, $11 trillion in swaps, and $7 trillion in options; $20 trillion are in interest rate derivatives, and $8 trillion in exchange derivatives. Chase, J. P. Morgan, City Bank, Nations Bank, and Citibank are some of the biggest U.S. bank holders of derivative contracts.

To perform their new function, risk management, banks have been shifting the focus of their organization from branch expansion and relations management to risk monitoring, measurement, and control. Banks have further shifted the focus of their personnel recruitment and retention policy from account executives and credit officers to financial engineers and rocket scientists imbued in mathematical and statistical models rather than in customer relations.

At the core of the new banking organization is the risk management department which, together with senior management, develops and implements risk management strategies:

- Writes risk management guidelines
- Sets risk tolerance levels, and approves risk measurement and risk control methods
- Devises risk monitoring procedures that allow senior management to assess its risk exposure to market risks
- Develops procedures to minimize the misuse of financial derivatives by bank traders and asset managers.

An introduction into banking risks and risk management in a globalizing economy, the remainder of the book takes a more detailed look at banking risks, their measurement, monitoring, and control, with emphasis on the use of financial derivatives to control three major banking risks: the interest rate, exchange rate, and credit risks that are at the core of banking business, in seven chapters. Chapter 2 begins with the definition of risk and the discussion of the different philosophical approaches to risk management and continues with the discussion of a number of risk management operational issues, such as banking risk identification and classification, banking risk measurement, monitoring, and control with on-balance sheet and off-balance sheet methods. Chapter 3 discusses the evolution of banking risk management and the banking environment and industry in the twentieth century. Particular attention is paid to the difference in risk management methods during the fragmented and highly regulated economy of the first three-quarters vis-à-vis the highly integrated global economy of the last quarter of the century. Chapter 4 reviews major financial derivative products: forwards, futures, option, caps, collars, and swaps, and their uses as risk management and speculation products. Chapter 5 discusses in more detail the management of credit risk. Particular attention is paid on an on-balance sheet risk management method, scoring, and rating, and on two off-balance sheet methods, credit options and credit swaps. Chapter 6 discusses in more detail the management of interest rate risk. Chapter 7 discusses in more detail the management of foreign currency risk, and Chapter 8 summarizes the discussion.

NOTES

1. Indeed, according to the U.S. Labor Department Handbook, between 1925 and 1973, the Consumer Price Index displayed a relatively small fluctuation. The same is true for interest rates after the 1933 banking regulations, and for the exchange rates after the 1947 Bretton Woods Accord.

2. According to the Board of the Federal Reserve System's 1982 *Historical Chart Book*, for the period 1940–1980, the number of U.S. banks remained roughly the same, while their branches increased from 4,000 in 1940 to 40,000 by 1980.

2

Banking Risk Management: An Overview

> Banks must manage risk more objectively, using quantitative skills to understand portfolio data and to predict portfolio performance. As a result, risk management will become more process-oriented and less dependent on individuals.
>
> Norman McClave (1996, 15)

Banking risk management is both a philosophical and an operational issue. As a philosophical issue, banking risk management is about attitudes toward risk and the payoff associated with it, and strategies in dealing with them. As an operational issue, risk management is about the identification and classification of banking risks, and methods and procedures to measure, monitor, and control them. Actually, the two approaches are not independent from one another. Attitudes toward risk shape up the guidelines for risk measurement, monitoring, and control.

An overview of banking risk management, this chapter is in two sections. The first section is a discussion of the philosophical approach to risk management, while the second section is a discussion of the operational approach to risk management.

BANKING RISK MANAGEMENT:
A PHILOSOPHICAL APPROACH

In everyday life, risk is about undesired, unpleasant, and at times disastrous prospective events associated with human action or inaction, accidents, such as earthquakes, poor judgment, and reckless behavior.

In the business and the investment community, risk is about probability distributions associated with the occurrence of unfavorable events, strikes, snow blizzards, technological breakdowns, and accidents in general that may adversely affect business activity and corporate performance. Risk is also about the probability of losses due to changes in the ideological, legal, and political regime that change the parameters of the game for a company, an industry, or the entire economy, resulting in loss of revenues or additional costs. The election of a pacifist government, for instance, may be followed by defense spending cuts, and the loss of contacts for defense contractors. The election of a pro-environmental government can impose additional costs on the chemical industry. The imposition of a business tax can result in a higher tax liability, while tighter affirmative action and gender legislation can impose additional costs to businesses.

Risk is also about the occurrence of certain economic events, such as fluctuations in input and output prices that also affect business and corporate performance. A sharp increase in energy prices, for instance, will have a negative impact on the utility, transportation, and the chemical industries that are heavy users of oil. A sharp rise in the price of grains will have a negative impact on the livestock industry and the cereal industry that use grains as a raw material. An increase in interest rates will have a negative impact on corporations that rely heavily on external financing for their working capital and investment needs. Likewise, a dollar appreciation will exert a negative impact on financial flows and balance sheets of multinational corporations. Thus, business risks may be general or systemic, affecting an entire industry, or unique, affecting one firm only:

Each company has its own unique set of constantly changing business risks. Certain risks will be external to the firm, many of which will be either difficult or impossible to control. Examples of these include competitor, financial markets or regulatory risk. Other will be internal, resulting from a company's own organization, processes, products, contractual commitments or relationships with customers, suppliers and employees. (Andersen 1995, 2)

Risk has a counterpart, a probability distribution of rewards associated with positive prospective events, when certain adverse events do not occur or certain favorable events do occur. The input and output price fluctuations mentioned earlier, for instance, can have a positive impact on a company's performance. A sharp decrease in the energy price will have a positive impact on utility, transportation, and the chemical industry. A decrease in interest rates will have a positive impact on corporations that rely on external financing for their capital needs, while a dollar depreciation will have a positive impact on the overseas income of U.S. multinational corporations.

In the banking industry and the investment community, risk is about all the factors that affect other industries. Yet as fiduciary institutions, these factors have a disproportionately greater impact on banks than on other businesses. Changes in the banking environment and industry structure have a negative effect on financial flows and net worth of individual banks. Economic downturns, for instance, would have a negative effect on the demand for new loans and loan repayments. Exchange or interest rate fluctuations would cause fluctuations in bank assets and liability positions.

Lending always involves some element of risk. These risks, which are most numerous and varied and which, in general, increase as the maturity of a loan increases, stem from those circumstances which result from the nonpayment of obligations when they come due. Some losses may result from "acts of God" such as storms, droughts, fire, earthquakes, and floods. The drop in the market value of raw materials and inventories is a hazard faced by all businesses. The possibility of a change in demand on the part of consumers or a technological change in productive and distributive methods may place some borrowers in the loss rather in the profit column. The price of securities in the organized or over-the-counter markets is subject to ups and downs. (Reed 1963, 210)

At the same time, the very factors that magnify banking risks have their own contigent counterpart, the probability distribution of desired changes that may result in gains. Changes in the banking environment, for instance, may have a positive impact on the banking industry. They may open up new markets, lower costs and allow the introduction of new products. Economic upturns will also have a positive impact on loan demand and payments.

Depending on a bank's financial position, interest rate and foreign currency fluctuations may have a negative or a positive impact on a bank's performance. Domestic currency appreciation would have a negative impact on foreign currency denominated assets and a positive impact on the foreign currency denominated liabilities. Conversely, interest rate increases will have a positive impact on floating interest rate-yielding assets and a negative impact on the floating rate liabilities.

The direct association between risks and rewards creates diverse attitudes among decision makers toward risks. Some decision makers love risks because they also love the rewards often associated with them. Others are indifferent toward risk because they are indifferent toward the rewards, while a third group is adverse to risk and is willing to forgo the rewards associated with it:

- Risk-loving are decision makers who like risk. When faced with two different reward/risk prospects, they choose the higher return/higher risk prospect.
- Risk-neutral are those decision makers who are indifferent toward risk-reward outcomes. Any risk-return choice-mix is consistent with their preferences.
- Risk-averse are those decision makers who dislike risk. When faced with the choice between two investments with different returns and degree of risks, they choose the investment with the lower risk and the lower return.

The diversity in decision-makers' attitudes toward risks creates diverse strategies toward risk management. Risk-neutral decision makers take a "passive," a "do nothing" approach; that is, they are prepared to accept any risk-reward mix. Risk-loving decision makers take an "active" approach; that is, they are willing to trade higher risk for higher rewards, and are prepared to commit resources to policies that serve this objective. Risk-averse decision makers also take an "active" approach; that is, they are willing to trade lower risk for lower rewards, and are prepared to commit resources to policies that serve this objective.

As is the case with other decision makers, bank decision makers have their own attitudes toward risk. Yet these attitudes are shaped by the banking environment and industry structure. Under multinationalization, a period of steady interest rates, the banking industry enjoyed a market sanctuary, bankers adopted risk neutral attitudes; that is, they took a "do nothing" approach toward interest rate and foreign exchange risks. At the same time, bankers adopted a risk-averse attitude toward liquidity, and especially credit risk, which they managed through close monitoring of deposits and loans, and close relations with corporate clients and central bankers (relationship banking).

Under globalization, one group of bankers took a risk-neutral attitude and a "do nothing" strategy; that is, they passively accepted the higher risk/reward world created by deregulation and market liberalization. Another group of bankers took a risk-loving attitude, especially toward interest rate risk, a strategy that resulted in aggressive expansion of unhedged balance sheet positions, and eventually to losses that contributed to banking crises. A third group of bankers took a risk-averse attitude, especially toward foreign exchange and interest rate risk, which led to the careful identification, monitoring, and control of banking risks, an issue to be addressed in the following section.

BANKING RISK MANAGEMENT: AN OPERATIONAL APPROACH

The operational approach to risk management begins with the identification and classification of banking risks and continues with their monitoring and control.

Identification and Classification of Banking Risks

As discussed earlier, under multinationalization and government regulation, banking risks were limited and a minor concern of management. Thus, there was no compelling reason to identify, measure, and manage risks, especially interest rate and foreign exchange risks.

The succession of multinationalization and regulation by globalization and deregulation in recent years and the spread of new technology have raised risks and turned them into a major issue in management. "Identifying and aggregating risks across multiple independent lines of business became a major issue for top management, since in the evolving organizational structure they themselves were no longer engaged in the day-to-day management of the business units but were dependent upon formal reporting mechanisms for operating information" (Kimball 1997, 24).

Identifying and aggregating risks also became important for government and international banking organizations, which have come up with different classifications of risk. The U.S. Comptroller's Office, for instance, classifies risks in nine categories: foreign exchange, interest rate, price, liquidity, credit, transaction, compliance, reputation, and strategic. The Federal Reserve Bank classifies risks in six categories: liquidity, market, credit, operation, legal, and reputation. The EU classifies risks as credit risk, liquidity risk, interest rate risk, foreign exchange risk, and so on.

In this book we classify financial risks into two categories, traditional and nontraditional (see Table 2.1).

Table 2.1
Banking Risks

Traditional Risks	Nontraditional Risks	
	Market Risks	Other Risks
Liquidity Risk	Interest Rate Risk	Commodity Price Risk
Credit Risk	Position Risk	Investment Portfolio Risk
Political and Legal Risk	Net Income Risk	Financial Derivatives Risk
Operation Risk	Foreign Exchange Risk	
	Conversion Risk	
	Position Risk	
	Liquidation Risk	

Traditional Banking Risks

Traditional banking risks are risks arising from the basic function of banks as intermediaries, that is, as borrowers, lenders, and investors of funds. Traditional banking risks can be classified in four categories, liquidity risk, credit risk, political and legal risk, and operation risk.

Liquidity Risk

Liquidity risk is simply a bank's inability to meet its daily payments. Specifically, liquidity risk is the probability of bank failure to fulfill its obligations and commitments to its depositors and borrowers. This probability, in turn, depends on industry and economy-wide factors (systemic risk), and bank specific risks. Liquidity risk arises on both sides of the balance bank sheet. On the liability side, liquidity risk is associated with the inability of banks to meet their obligations to their depositors, especially in periods of massive deposit withdrawals caused by the lack of confidence of the public in the industry. On the asset side, liquidity risk is associated with banks' failure to satisfy demand for new loans, advances or facilities, and raise funds for new investment opportunities.

Simply put, liquidity risk is about the probability of a bank failing to hold sufficient liquid assets to meet liquid liabilities, which in turn, depends on the mismatch of asset and liability maturity (maturity gap). A bank with a large portion of long-term assets and a large portion of short-term liabilities assumes a high liquidity risk. Conversely, a bank with a small portion of long-term assets and a small portion of long-term liabilities assumes a low liquidity risk. Ideally, a bank with a perfect maturity match of its assets and liabilities is immune to liquidity risk.

Credit Risk

Credit risk is the prospect of a bank failing to collect principal and income from both loan and investment positions. This prospect, in turn, depends on the maturity length of the loan and investment positions, on a number of borrower-specific factors, and industry and economywide factors (systemic risk).

Liquidity and credit risks are not independent from one another. An increase in the credit risk will also increase liquidity risk. The inability of a bank to collect on loans will have an impact on its ability to meet its deposit obligations, especially in periods of massive bank failures that cause panics among depositors, accelerating withdrawals.

Political and Legal Risks

The political and legal risks are risks associated with changes in political and legal banking environment, such as riots, terrorist attacks, government shake-ups, new regulation, and failure to enforce contracts, which may directly or indirectly affect the performance of individual banks.

Operation Risk

Operation risk is the risk associated with the day-to-day banking operations. A computer glitch, a personnel shortage, fraud, a strike, a service failure, brand erosion, an accident, or even bad weather can disturb banking operations and earnings. Operation risk is particularly high for large-scale banks and for banks that rely on high technology and specialized personnel to deliver complex products, such as financial derivatives.

Nontraditional Banking Risks

Nontraditional risks are risks associated with the liberalization of foreign exchange and domestic financial markets, the domestic and overseas expansion of banks and their venturing to the other segments of the financial service industry, and the invasion of the banking industry by other segments of the financial service sector. Nontraditional banking risks include market risks and other risks.

Market Risks

Market risks are risks arising from changes in financial market conditions that may affect the value of financial instruments, and, therefore, the net income and net worth of banking institutions. Market risks include interest rate risk, foreign exchange risk, and the liquidation risk.

Interest Rate Risk

Interest rate risk is associated with unexpected and unfavorable fluctuations in interest rates that may negatively affect both the price of bank assets and the income derived from these assets:

- Net income or return risk is the risk associated with a decline in the bank's net financial flows due to changes in interest rates.
- Position risk is the risk arising from a decline in the value of the banks' net worth due to a change in interest rates.

The size of interest rate risk depends on the following:

- The asset and liability mismatch, the gap between the interest rate-sensitive assets and the interest rate-sensitive liabilities (net income risk).
- The direction and the percentage in the change of interest rate (position risk).

The interest rate risk is illustrated in the simplified balance sheet and the operations of Bank XYZ:

Assets		Liabilities	
Treasury note	$1,000,000	CDs	$800,000
		Equity	$200,000

Assuming that the treasury note matures in three years and pays a 14-percent coupon, and the CD matures in a year and pays a 10-percent return, the annual operations statement is as follows:

Treasury Note Revenues	$140,000
CD Expenses	$80,000
Profit	$60,000

Assuming that the three-year bond yield rates rise by 2 percent to 16 percent, the price of the note will decline to $955,082, which is estimated as follows:

$$P = 140,000 \sum_{t=1}^{3} [1/(1 + 0.16)^t] + 1,000,000 * 1/(1 + 0.16)^3 = \$955,082$$

So, the balance sheet becomes as follows:

Assets		Liabilities	
Treasury Note	$955,082	CD	$800,000
		Equity	$155,082

Thus, an increase in interest rates by 200-basis points resulted in a decrease in the price of the note by $44,018, which led in a decline of the bank's net worth (position risk) by the same amount. As the CD is renewed annually, the operations statement remains the same, that is, the interest rate income risk was zero.

If in the second operation period, when the CD is due for renewal deposit rates have also been raised by 2 percent, to 12 percent and treasury notes rates remain at 16 percent, the operations statement will look as follows:

Treasury Note Revenues	$140,000
CD Expenses	$96,000
Profit	$44,000

The balance sheet is as follows:

Assets		Liabilities	
Treasury Note	$967,894	CD	$960,000
		Equity	$167,894

Thus, compared with the first year, the rise in interest rates had a negative impact on both the invested principal (position risk) and on income (income risk). Specifically, operating income fell by $16,000 and the net worth by $32,106.

The treasury note price is as follows:

$$P = 140,000 \sum_{t=1}^{3} [1/(1 + 0.16)^t] + 1,000,000 * 1/(1 + 0.16)^2 = \$967,894$$

Thus, the initial balance sheet of the bank under consideration displays a positive interest rate gap, that is, the long positions exceed the short positions that are interest rate-sensitive. The results would had been different if the interest rate gap was negative, an issue to be addressed later.

In short, the impact of unexpected interest rate fluctuations on bank income and net worth depends on the structure of its balance sheet, namely on the portion of interest-sensitive assets and liabilities and their maturity length, which will be discussed in the second section.

Foreign Exchange Risk

As the term suggests, foreign exchange rate risk is associated with unexpected and unfavorable fluctuations of foreign currency exchange rates that may have a negative effect on the value of financial flows and net worth of the foreign currency-denominated assets and liabilities of banking institutions. A devaluation of the foreign currency against the domestic currency, for instance, would undermine the value of the foreign currency denominated assets and flows. The total gains or losses depend on the short or long position (open position) in each foreign currency and the size of the movement of the specific currency. A sharp devaluation of the dollar against the yen, for instance, will increase the value of U.S. banks' yen-denominated assets, and the value of bank earnings from those assets.

Foreign exchange rate risk can be classified in two categories:

1. Conversion or position foreign exchange risk; that is, risk associated with open foreign currency-denominated asset or liability positions.
2. Transaction or net income risk; that is, risk associated with the conversion of certain consolidated balance sheet items for banks that are engaged in overseas operations.

Liquidation Risk

Liquidation risk arises from the difficulty of credit institutions to liquidate an investment position. A foreign debt moratorium, for instance, like that imposed by Russia on foreign debt in the fall of 1998, makes it difficult or even impossible for credit institutions that hold debt in that country to close their positions. Capital movement restrictions like those imposed by the Malaysian government in the aftermath of the 1998 Asian crisis also make it difficult for banks to close their positions in those countries. Depressed real estate markets like those of the United States in the late 1980s and Japan in the mid-1990s are yet another two cases in point. Sometimes, liquidation risk may arise because of thinly traded assets, like over the counter equities, or junk debt.

Other Risks

Other risks arise from fluctuations of commodity prices, equity prices, and derivative price that may directly or indirectly affect bank performance.

Commodity Price Risks

Commodity price risks are risks associated with unexpected commodity price fluctuations that may have a direct or indirect negative effect on a bank's net income and net worth. Unexpected oil price declines in the early 1980s, for instance, had a devastating impact on the Southwest U.S. real estate market resulting in loan defaults and bank failures. Real estate price declines in the mid-1990s had also a devastating effect on the Japanese and other Asian banks.

Investment Portfolio Risks

Investment portfolio risks are associated with unexpected and unfavorable fluctuations in equity prices that may affect, both directly and indirectly, bank performance. Sharp equity price declines, for instance, will result in direct losses for banks' long equity positions. Equity price declines will also affect the net worth of bank clients and eventually their ability to borrow or repay existing loans. Precipitous equity declines may also result in a recession, leading to massive bankruptcies and loan defaults and bank failures.

Financial Derivative Risks

Financial derivative risks are associated with unexpected and unfavorable movements in the price of financial derivatives, especially when used as speculative devices. The writing of "naked" calls, for instance, can result in severe losses, when the market moves in the opposite direction than the one bet during the life of the option. The failure of one party to stand up to its contractual obligation can also result in financial losses for the other party (counterpart risk), and may create a chain reaction in the financial service industry, resulting in several derivative contract defaults (systemic risk).

Thus, depending on the source, banking risks fall into two categories, traditional risks, arising from the traditional function of banks as financial intermediaries, and nontraditional risks, arising with the transformation of the industry into "one-stop" shops for financial products and investment management services. Nontraditional risks can be further classified into market risks and other risks.

Though presented separately, banking risks are interdependent. An increase in credit risk, for instance, can increase the size of non-performing loans, which in turn will raise liquidity risk. An increase in market risk, like a sharp increase in exchange rates or interest rates can, in turn, depress real estate values and raise the risk of default of real estate borrowers; that is, raise credit risks, which complicates risk measurement.

Risk Measurement

As discussed earlier, for years, risk, especially market risk, has been a minor factor in business management, and its measurement drew little attention from the academic and the consulting community. In addition, attained to local economy and most notably to well-established corporate clients, bank managers relied on personal relations and experience and simple credit analysis techniques to assess the risk of their clients, an issue to be further addressed in the next chapter.

Nowadays, as risk has turned from a minor to a major factor in business management, risk measurement has attracted a great deal of attention both from academia and the consulting industry, which have developed a number of individual and aggregate risk measures (see Table 2.2).

Single Risk Measures

As the term suggests, single risk measures focus on the separate measurement of the impact of each individual risk on a bank's net income and net worth. Duration and Gap Analysis, for instance, measure interest rate risk, FX Sensitivity Analysis measures foreign exchange risk and beta measure portfolio risk (see Table 2.2). Each measure has its own advantages and disadvantages.

Table 2.2
Single and Aggregate Risk Measures

Type of Measure	Focus on	Instrument (Method of measure)	Risk Measured
Single	Individual Risk	Portfolio Standard Deviation, σ	Investment Risk
		Relative Variation, β	Investment Risk
		Gap Analysis	Interest rate: Income risk
		Duration	Interest rate: Position risk
		Convexity	Interest rate: Position risk
		FX Sensitivity Analysis	Foreign Exchange risk
		Liquidity Ratio Analysis Maturity Gap	Liquidity risk
		Credit Rating (Ranking)	Credit Risk
Aggregate	Global Risk	VAR	Total Risk
		Total Risk Management	Total Risk

Liquidity Risk

As discussed earlier, liquidity risk is the probability of a bank failing to fulfill its obligations to its customers, stemming from the mismatch of bank financial flows, that is, deposits and income vis-à-vis withdrawals and operational expenses. Liquidity risk is particularly high when depositors lose confidence in a banking institution or the banking industry as a whole. Liquidity risk is also high in periods of financial crisis like a stock market crisis, when the demand for liquidity is unusually high.

Liquidity risk is measured in two ways, with conventional Liquidity Ratio Analysis and with modern Gap Analysis or Maturity Ladder.

Conventional Methods: Liquidity Ratio Analysis

Liquidity Ratio Analysis applies a number of ratios to measure and monitor a bank's liquid assets vis-à-vis liquid liabilities.

- Cash/Deposit ratio = Cash/Demand and savings deposits
- Cash/Total deposits
- Cash plus government securities/Demand and time deposits
- Cash plus government securities/Total deposits
- High liquid assets/Demand and time deposits
- High liquid assets/Total deposits
- Receivables from other banks/Payables to other banks
- Cash plus high liquid assets/Maturing liabilities

Banks with low liquidity ratios, that is, below those of the industry, have a higher probability of running into liquidity problems than banks with high liquidity ratios. In either case, a bank's liquidity needs may vary from time to time, and, therefore, liquidity ratio's must be calculated separately for each time period.

Modern Methods: Maturity Gap or Maturity Ladder

Maturity Ladder is a more detailed measure of a bank's asset and liability maturity mismatch. Specifically, the method classifies a bank's assets and liabilities into maturity zones, beginning with the overnight zone and ending with longer periods of more than a year. Thus, the excess or deficiency liquidity of each time zone and the accumulated excess or deficiency for more than one zone is estimated (potential and actual) as described in Table 2.3.[1]

Maturity Ladder tables allow banks to recalculate liquidity ratios for each time zone separately, and therefore develop a more accurate measure of its liquidity position:

$$\text{Liquidity of each zone} = \frac{\text{Zone's Total Payable}}{\text{Zone's Total Excess or Deficiency}}$$

Table 2.3
Maturity Ladder for a Representative Bank (Million $)

| | TIME ZONES | | | | | | | |
| | DAYS | | | | | YEARS | | |
	Over-night	2-7	8-30	31-180	181-365	1-2	2-3	More than 3 years
Assets	500	250	200	250	400	300	100	100
Liabilities	400	350	250	200	200	350	200	150
Difference	+100	- 100	-50	+50	+200	-50	-100	-50
Interest Receivable	10	25	40	85	110	30	25	35
Interest Payable	8	28	22	115	120	20	21	30
Difference	+2	-3	+18	-30	-10	+10	+4	+5
Off balance sheet receivables	0	5	8	40	32	28	30	20
Off balance sheet Payables	0	2	5	55	43	25	10	10
Difference	0	+3	+3	-15	-11	+3	+20	+10
TOTAL EXCESS OR DEFICIENCY	+102	-100	-19	+5	+179	-37	-76	-35
DEFICIENCY	+102	+2	- 17	-12	+ 167	+130	+54	+19

Total liquidity ratio for each time zone equals accumulated excess or deficiency liquidity from all time zones. Under normal circumstances, the total liquidity ratio for zones 8–30, and 31–180 is –17, and –12, which means that the bank has a liquidity problem.

In short, liquidity risk can be measured in two ways, with single ratio analysis that provides a general assessment of a bank's ability to fulfill its obligations to its customers, and with multiple-ratio analysis, such as Maturity Ladder that provides a specific assessment of a bank's liquidity for each separate zone.

Credit Risk

As discussed earlier, credit risk is the probability of banks failing to collect on their loans and investments. Thus, credit risk is closely connected with the quantity and quality of bank loan and investment portfolio; that is, the credit worthiness of current and prospective clients, monitored and measured by ratio analysis.

Ratio Analysis

Ratio analysis applies a number of criteria that determine the credit worthiness of the borrower, which can be classified into primary and secondary criteria. Primary criteria establish the customer's funding needs, determine its economic and financial position, and evaluate the profitability, efficiency, and the quality of its organization. Primary criteria can be classified into quantitative and qualitative.

Quantitative criteria establish the customer's need for financing and evaluate its economic and financial performance:

Establish the financing need	Credit line
	Financing from other banks
	Residual financing
Economic position	Sales growth/Market share
	Performance
	Projections
Financial position	Net worth
	Debt and debt ratios
	Short-term
	Long-term
	Liquidity

Current ratio
Quick ratio
Working capital
Profitability
Return on equity
Total return
Profit margin
Efficiency
Receivables turnover
Payments turnover
Inventory turnover
Cash flows
Operational
Other
Total
Reserves

Qualitative criteria profile the vision, organizational structure, and the intangible assets of the client.

Management and Organization (Decision-Making Structure, Information Structure, Communication Structure)

- Personnel (education, experience, ability, relations with management)
- Capital equipment and technology
- Competitive advantages
- Flexibility and adaptability
- Investment/modernization
- Vision (mission and core values)
- Reputation
- Previous financing and cooperation performance
- Types of financing (short-term versus long-term)
- Use of risk management techniques

Secondary criteria provide additional information about the customer's position to repay:

- Collateral offered
- Guarantees

- Previous financing and cooperation
- Type of financing (short-term versus long-term)
- Use of risk management techniques
- Social criteria

In short, credit risk is measured with a number of criteria that determine the ability and the will of borrowers to repay income and principal, an issue to be further discussed in Chapter 5.

Interest Rate Risk

As discussed earlier, interest rate risk is the prospect of a bank suffering financial losses due to unexpected and unfavorable interest rate fluctuations. Such losses are in turn classified into income and position risks. Position risk is measured in two ways, Duration, and Convexity. Income interest rate risk is measured with Gap Analysis.

Position Interest Rate Risk: Duration Analysis

Duration Analysis measures the position exposure component of interest rate risk; that is, the changes in the value of a bank's portfolio or single investment position due to a small parallel change in interest rates. Thus, Duration is the slope of the expected value of a financial product or portfolio with respect to the interest rates. The larger the duration of the bank portfolio or product, the more interest rate sensitive the product is. Conversely, the smaller the duration of the product, the less interest rate sensitive the product or portfolio is.

Put in another way, duration is the average time it takes for a finance product to complete its income payments. Duration is closely related to the concept of maturity; that is, the time it takes for a financial asset to complete all its income payments, but with the exception of the case of the zero-coupon bonds, maturity and duration are two different concepts. The maturity and the maturity of a four-year zero-coupon bond and a four-year coupon bond is a case in point. Though both securities mature in four years (their duration) the average time it takes to complete their income payment differs. The zero-coupon bond makes its payments at the end of the four-year period, while the coupon bond spreads its payments over the four-year period. Thus, the average time (duration) of payment flows of the coupon bond is shorter than the duration of the zero-coupon bond. As a result, the coupon bond is less sensitive to interest rate changes, an issue that will be further addressed.

The first attempts to measure duration date back in the late 1930s to Frederick Macaulay's formula, which weighs the expected income flows of a financial asset by the time periods they accrue to their holders. In this sense, Macaulay's duration or Simple Duration (SD) measures the average time it takes for an asset to accrue its income payments.

More recently, statisticians came up with a Modified Duration (MD) of Macaulay's formula, which measures, with high approximation, the percentage change in the price of the financial asset in response to a certain change in the asset yield. Thus, Modified Duration is the interest-rate elasticity of the price of a security instrument.

Formally, the Simple Duration can be calculated as the weighted average of the discounted income flows of an investment product:

$$SD = \frac{\dfrac{P_1}{(1+r)} * 1 + \dfrac{P_2}{(1+r)^2} * 2 + , \ldots , + \dfrac{P_n}{(1+r)^n} * n}{\dfrac{P_1}{(1+r)} + \dfrac{P_2}{(1+r)^2} + , \ldots , + \dfrac{P_n}{(1+r)^n}} \tag{1}$$

or

$$SD = \frac{\dfrac{t\,P\,t}{(1+r)^t}}{\dfrac{Pt}{(1+r)^n}} \tag{2}$$

or

$$SD = \frac{t\,PV\,t}{PVt} \tag{3}$$

where

r = Interest (required rate of return or yield to maturity)

P_1 = First period payments (revenue interest–interest payments)

P_2 = Second period payments, and so on

n = Number of periods

t = Specific time period

PVt = Present value of payment at period t

The value of a security's Duration is determined by several factors. First, the level of the security's interest rates (coupons): the larger the coupons, the lower the value of Duration. Second, the maturity date of the security: the longer the maturity, the higher the value of the Duration. Third, Duration is inversely related to market yields: the higher the market yields, the lower the duration. Fourth, the size and the frequency of income payments: the larger the size and the frequency of income payments: the lower the Duration. For example, let us take a three-year bond with a face value of $1,000,000, paying a coupon of $100,000. What is its Duration?

$$SD = \frac{\dfrac{100{,}000}{(1.10)} * 1 + \dfrac{100{,}000}{(1.10)^2} * 2 + \dfrac{100{,}000 + 1{,}000{,}000}{(1.10)^3} * 3}{\dfrac{100{,}000}{(1.10)} + \dfrac{100{,}000}{(1.110)^2} + \dfrac{100{,}000 + 1{,}000{,}000}{(1.10)^3}}$$

$$= \frac{90{,}909 + 165{,}289 + 2{,}479{,}339}{90{,}909 + 82{,}645 + 826{,}446} = \frac{2{,}735{,}534}{1{,}000{,}000} = 2.735$$

Assuming that the yield of the security of the previous example rises to 14 percent, the SD will be as follows:

$$SD = \frac{\dfrac{100{,}000}{(1.14)} * 1 + \dfrac{100{,}000}{(1.14)^2} * 2 + \dfrac{100{,}000 + 1{,}000{,}000}{(1.14)^3} * 3}{\dfrac{100{,}000}{(1.14)} + \dfrac{100{,}000}{(1.14)^2} + \dfrac{100{,}000 + 1{,}000{,}000}{(1.14)^3}}$$

$$= \frac{2,468,996}{907,126} = 2.721$$

Thus, as interest rate increase by two basis points, the security's Duration falls from 2.735 to 2.721.

Assuming that the bond's income flow payments are independent of interest rate fluctuations, the following formula provides the Modified Duration (MD):

$$MD = \frac{SD}{1 + r}$$

where

SD = Simple Duration
  r = Yield
MD = Modified Duration

Let us assume a five-year $1,000,000 note paying a 12-percent coupon, which for the examined period is equal to the yield to maturity. The following two procedures provide an illustration of the difference between Simple Duration and Modified Duration.

Procedure 1: Consider the financial flows in Table 2.4

SD = Weighted Present Value/Present Value

  = 4,037,000/1,000,000

  = 4.037

where

Weighted Present Value = Period * Present Value

$$MD = SD/1 + r = 4.037 / 1.12 = 3.60$$

Procedure 2: An alternative calculation procedure illustrated in Table 2.5 sums up the weighted financial flows to the total present value.

Proportion of Flows (Column 4) = 1,000,000 / Flows Present Value

$$MD = SD/1 + r = 3.60$$

Table 2.4
Simple and Modified Duration Calculations

1	2	3	4	5	6
Period	Financial Flows	Present Value	Weighted Present Value	Simple Duration	Modified Duration
1	120,000	107,143	107,143		
2	120,000	95,663	191,326	4,037,350 /	SD /
3	120,000	85,414	256,242	1,000,000	1+r
4	120,000	76,261	305,044		
5	1,120,000	635,519	3,177,595		
		1,000,000	4,037,350	4.037	3.60

Table 2.5
Alternative Simple and Modified Duration Calculations

1	2	3	4	5	6
Period	Financial Flows	Flows Present Value	Proportion of Flows	Weighted Proportion (4*1)	Modified Duration
1	120,000	107,143	0.107143	0.107143	
2	120,000	95,663	0.9095663	0.191326	SD/
3	120,000	85,414	0.085417	0.256242	1+r
4	120,000	76,261	0.076261	0.305044	
5	1,120,000	635,519	0.635617	3.177595	
		1,000,000	1	4.037 (Simple Duration)	3.60

Moreover, for two securities of the same maturity and interest rate but of different number of payments, the security with the smaller number of payments has the larger duration; that is, the five-year coupon bond has a smaller duration than a five-year zero-coupon bond.

To further illustrate this point, Table 2.6 calculates the Simple and the Modified Duration for a five-year zero-coupon bond, yielding a 12-percent return, paid at the end of its maturity period.

In short, as it is indicated from Table 2.6, the modified durations of the two financial products are as follows:

$$\text{Coupon Bond} = 3.60$$

$$\text{Zero-Coupon Bond} = 4.46$$

Thus the price of the zero-coupon bond is more sensitive to interest rate fluctuations. A 1-percent increase in interest rates will be followed by a change of 3.60 percent and 4.46 percent in the corre-

Table 2.6
Zero-Coupon Bond, Simple and Modified Duration

1	2	3	4	5	6
Period	Financial Flows	Flows Present Value	Weighted Present Value	Simple Duration	Modified Duration
1	0	0	0		
2	0	0	0	2,837,134.3/	SD/
3	0	0	0	567,426.85	1+r
4	0	0	0		
5	1,000,000	567,426.85	2,837,134.3		
				5	4.46

sponding coupon bond and zero-coupon bond prices. Thus, since, on average, the coupon bond makes payments faster than the zero-coupon bond, the coupon bond has a lower interest rate risk.

In short, duration is the slope or the first derivative of the present value of a financial product with respect to the interest rate. Thus, duration is accurate only for small changes in interest rates (one-to-two basis points), but inaccurate for large interest rate changes, and must be supplemented by convexity.

Convexity

Convexity measures the curvature of the value profile of a fixed income security. Thus, convexity is the second derivative of the value of a financial product with respect to the interest rates; that is, it measures how the elasticity itself changes as interest rate changes. The larger the curvature of the value profile of the security, the less accurate duration is as an indication of the interest rate-sensitivity of the value of a security; and the smaller the convexity, the more accurate the duration. Thus, convexity should be applied together with duration to measure interest rate risks, especially for a large (several basis points) interest rate fluctuation.

In either case, duration and convexity measure position risk; that is, the impact of interest rate fluctuations on the expected value of a security, while the impact of interest rate fluctuations on the bank income is measured with gap analysis.

Interest Rate Income Risk: Gap Analysis

As the term suggests, gap analysis measures the gap of rate-sensitive assets and rate-sensitive liabilities at a given point in time. A bank, for instance, which issues a six-month CD and applies the funds for the purchase of a two-year treasury note will experience a net interest income decline if interest rates rise after the CD matures at the end of the sixth month because it will be rolled over at a higher rate, while it will continue to collect the same interest rate on the two-year treasury note.

Formally, gap is the difference between the value of the long positions (assets) and the short positions (liabilities) of a bank's portfolio that are interest rate sensitive:

Gap = Value of Interest Rate Sensitive Long Positions
　　　 − Value of Interest Rate Sensitive Short Positions

To determine the bank exposure to interest rate fluctuations, bank assets and liabilities must be classified according to their maturity or their interest rate renewal time, whichever of the two comes first, and according to the type of interest rate paid or earned, that is, fixed or floating. A positive gap means that the bank has a larger asset than liability-interest exposure to interest rate risk, that is, long exposure.

Assets	Liabilities
	Capital $2,000
Non-Interest Rate-Sensitive Assets $4,000	Non-Interest Rate-Sensitive Liabilities $5,000
Interest Rate-Sensitive Assets $6,000	Interest Rate-Sensitive Liabilities $3,000

Interest Rate Gap = +3,000

A negative gap means that the bank has a larger liability exposure to interest rate risk, that is, short exposure.

Assets	Liabilities
	Capital $2,000
Non-Interest Rate–Sensitive Assets $7,000	Non-Interest Rate–Sensitive Liabilities $2,000
Interest Rate–Sensitive Assets $3,000	Interest Rate–Sensitive Liabilities $6,000

Interest Rate Gap = −3,000

The change in revenues can be measured as follows:

Revenues = (Interest Sensitive Assets * Interest Rate Change)
           − (Interest Sensitive Liabilities * Interest Rate Change)

or

Revenues = Gap * Interest Rate Change

The impact of interest rate fluctuations on revenues depends on the bank's interest gap. A bank with a positive interest rate gap, for instance, will experience a net interest revenue rise if interest rates rise, since more assets than liabilities will be subject to an increase in the interest rate. If interest rates on both assets and liabilities rise by two basis points, net income will rise by $60 ($120 − $60). The same bank will experience a net interest rate income loss if interest rates decline. Conversely, a bank with a negative interest rate gap will experience interest rate income increase if interest rates fall, and a net income decline if interest rates rise. If interest rates drop by 2 percent, net income will rise by $60.

In short, gap analysis is an estimate of a bank's interest rate income risk exposure; that is, it measures the impact of interest rate changes to the bank's net income. But it has two drawbacks, it focuses only on one period, and cannot be compared with that of other banks, which are overcome by the cumulative gap and the relative gap index.

The cumulative gap measures the interest rate sensitiveness of the balance sheet when the maturity of both asset and liabilities components and their interest rate renewal time are taken into consideration; that is, it examines several rather than one maturity period.

Assuming that the bank has detailed information on maturity days for every asset and liability, its cumulative gap is calculated in Table 2.7. As is indicated by the table for the first three periods, the bank has a negative interest rate gap, and therefore, an interest rate decline will have a positive effect on its revenues, while for the next three periods, the bank has a positive interest rate gap,

Table 2.7
Cumulative Gap ($ Millions)

Renewal Period	Assets	Liabilities	Gap	Cumulative Gap
Overnight	15	26	(11)	(11)
1-30 days	10	16	(6)	(17)
30-90 days	20	24	(4)	(21)
90-180 days	25	14	11	10
180-365 days	15	11	4	6
1-5 years	11	6	5	1
Over 5 years	6	5	1	0
Total	102	102		0

and therefore, an increase in interest rates will have a positive effect on its revenues.

The relative gap measures the ratio of interest-sensitive assets to interest-sensitive liabilities, and therefore it is offered for comparisons with similar banks in the industry:

$$\text{Relative Gap} = (\text{Interest-Sensitive Assets} / \text{Interest-Sensitive Liabilities}) * 100$$

A ratio greater than 50 percent means that assets are more interest rate sensitive than liabilities. Conversely, a ratio less than 50 percent means that assets are less interest rate sensitive than liabilities.

In short, a bank's exposure to interest rate risk can be measured in three ways. Duration and convexity, which measure the interest rate position risk, and gap analysis, which measure the interest rate income risk. Both measures are used for interest rate risk management, an issue addressed in Chapter 7.

Foreign Exchange Risk

As discussed earlier, foreign exchange risk is the income or capital loss due to unfavorable changes in the foreign exchange rate that eventually affect negatively the net worth of a bank. Foreign exchange risk exists in any investment or transaction involving foreign exchange; that is, currency transaction between domestic currency and any foreign currency or cross-currency transactions.

Foreign exchange risk is measured with FX sensitivity analysis or FX gap analysis, which calculates the foreign exchange sensitivity of "on-balance sheet" and "off-balance sheet" positions.

To apply this method, banks and financial institutions should know their open-short and long-open foreign currency positions.[2] Specifically, the method includes five steps:

1. Calculation of the on- and off-balance sheet long and short positions for each currency.
2. Calculation of the difference between long and short positions for each currency; that is, calculation of the net position for each currency.
3. Formulation of exchange rate forecasting scenarios.
4. Calculation of profits and losses for each exchange rate forecast scenario.
5. Estimation of profits and losses for each currency by multiplying the expected change in each currency and the net position in that currency.

Thus, FX sensitivity analysis focuses on the impact of foreign currency fluctuations on the net position of the bank in each currency and for each financial product denominated in the same currency; that is, the difference between the value of the long positions and the short positions in that product:

Net Position of Financial Product X = Value Long Positions
− Value of Short Positions

The total net position in the specific currency is the sum of all net positions of each specific financial product (on- and off-balance sheet) denominated in that currency, which can be long or short.

The final net position, in turn, determines the currency impact on the bank's net income:

Change in Income = (Long Positions * FX Price Change)
− (Short Positions * FX Price Change)

or

Change in Income = Net Position * FX Price Change

The relationship between net position, foreign exchange rate fluctuations, and income are summarized in Table 2.8.

Table 2.8
Foreign Exchange Price Fluctuations, Net Positions, and Income Changes

Net Position	Foreign Exchange Rate Fluctuations	
	Rise (Domestic currency devalued)	Decline (Domestic currency appreciated)
Long	Income Rise	Income Falls
Short	Income Falls	Income Rise
Zero or no Position	Income not affected	Income not affected

For example, bank C, an American Bank, on October 1, 1999 has positions in German Mark (DM), French Franc (FRF) and Japanese Yen (JPY) as follows:

Short-term loans to commercial companies, FRF denominated, total volume of FRF 5,000,0000 (long position)

Loan raised in Interbank market FRF 2,000,000 (short position)

Bank bond issued in German market DM 3,000,000 (short position)

Bought forward contract in a forward DM/$ price higher than spot, DM 5,000,000 (long position)

Issued letter of credit DM 4,000,000 (short position)

Certificate of deposit issued in the Japanese market JPY 50,000,000 (short position)

Long-term, JPY-denominated loans JPY 20,000,000

Participation in JPY-denominated syndicated loan with JPY 30,000,000 (long position)

The projected changes in the prices of these three currencies against the dollar are the following:

FRF/$ − 0.2 ($ price increase or $ appreciation)

DM/$ 0.1 ($ price decrease or $ devalued)

JPY/$ − 0.02 ($ price increase)

According to these changes in the foreign currencies prices will have an impact on the bank's income as illustrated in Table 2.9.

Thus, a 20-cent dollar appreciation against FRF will result in a $600,000 income losses; and a 10-cent dollar appreciation against the DM will result in a $200,000 in losses.

In short, the FX analysis provides banks with an estimate of FX risk, a prerequisite for FX risk, an issue to be further addressed in Chapter 7.

Investment Portfolio Risk

Variance and Beta

Markowitz's portfolio selection model begins with the recognition of uncertainty as a "silent feature" of investing. As Markowitz puts it: "Uncertainty is a feature of security investment. Economic forces are not understood well enough to be beyond doubt or error. Even if the consequences of economic conditions were understood

Table 2.9
Application of Foreign Exchange Price Fluctuations, Net FX Positions, and Income Changes (In U.S. Dollars)

Currency	Long Positions	Short Positions	Net Positions	Projected Price Change	Income Change
FRF	5,000,000	2,000,000	Long 3,000,000	-0,2	-600,000
DEM	5,000,000	7,000,000	Short - 2,000,000	0,1	-200,000
JPY	50,000,000	50,000,000	0	- 0,01	0
				TOTAL	-800,000

perfectly, non-economic influences can change the course of general prosperity, the level of market, or the success of a particular security."[3] Markowitz, in turn, came up with a measurement of portfolio volatility, the standard deviation of the returns of its assets. Then, he posed the question: Why will people assume risks? Some people simply will not. They will stay with low-return, risk-free investments. Yet others will reach to the financial markets and assume some risks of losing part or all of the invested principal in anticipation of higher returns. In fact, the higher the risk, the fewer the people willing to assume risks for the higher return. In other words, different individuals have different attitudes, different degrees of tolerance toward risk and returns, as discussed earlier in the chapter.

Assuming that the average investor is risk averse, it will take a higher return to entice them to invest in risky assets; and the higher the risk, the higher the risk premium. Intermediate term bonds, for instance, command a risk premium over treasury bills and common stocks (see Figure 2.1). Markowitz further argued that, as long as portfolio securities are not perfectly correlated, portfolio diversification can lower risks. "While the return on a diversified portfolio will be equal to the average of the rates of return on its individual holdings, its volatility will be less than the volatility of its individual holdings."[4] Simply put, the aggregate risk of a portfolio is less than the sum of individual risks.

At this point, it must be emphasized that portfolio diversification can reduce security-specific risk, not the systematic or market risk; that is, portfolio diversification has its own limits (see Figure 2.2).

How volatile is a portfolio compared to the rest of the market? Addressing this question, Markowitz's student William Sharpe developed a relative-risk measurement model, the Capital Asset

Figure 2.1
Risk versus Return: Riskier Assets Command Higher Return

Return (%)

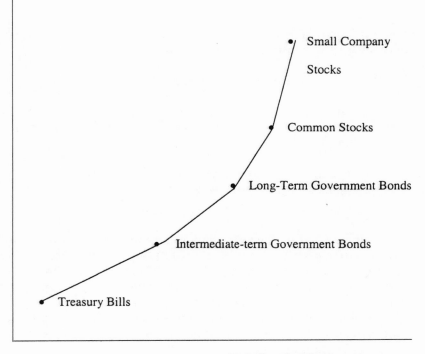

Risk (Standard Deviation)

Figure 2.2
Portfolio Diversification and Volatility

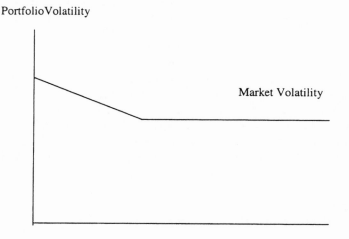

Pricing Model, also known as β (beta), which measures the portfolio volatility in relation to market volatility:

β = Portfolio volatility/market volatility

Depending on the size of this indicator, some portfolios are more volatile, some as volatile, and others less volatile than the rest of the market:

β > 1 portfolio more volatile than the rest of the market
β = 1 portfolio as volatile as the rest of the market
β < 1 portfolio less volatile than the rest of the market

Markowitz's and Sharpe's models provide valuable instruments for measuring both absolute and relative portfolio risk. They contributed to the understanding of basic differences between systemic and diversifiable risk. Specifically, the two models allow investors to implement certain investment objectives, control the components of portfolio volatility, and to improve efficiency. But they have two limitations, instability and ambiguity. As Michaud puts it

In practice, the most important limitations of Mean Value (MV) Optimization are instability and ambiguity. MV optimizers function as chaotic investment decision system. Small changes in input assumptions often imply large changes in the optimized portfolio. Consequently, portfolio optimality is often not well defined. The procedure overuses statistically estimated information and magnifies the impact of estimation errors. (Michaud 1998, 3)

In short, individual-risk measures estimate the separate impact of different risks on a bank's balance sheet or operations statement. Thus, they require the identification and monitoring of each risk, a problem that is bypassed by aggregate risk measures.

Aggregate Risk Measures

As discussed earlier, aggregate risk measures are comprehensive risk measures; that is, they aggregate the impact of unexpected events on a bank's on- and off-balance sheet position, irrespective of the source of that fluctuation. Two broadly used measures are the Value at Risk (VAR), and the Total Risk Model (TRM).

VAR and TRM

VAR is simply a probability assessment of the potential losses that the bank is prepared to accept due to adverse market conditions (market risk) during a given time period. In this sense, VAR is an educated prediction about the potential losses from an investment position over a specified period of time, due to adverse price movements. In statistical terms, VAR is an estimate of a confidence interval that gives the probability of potential losses from an investment position.

VAR is estimated in three steps:

1. The calculation of the current portfolio value by multiplying portfolio positions by their current market prices.
2. The calculation of the distribution of changes to the portfolio values by multiplying portfolio positions with a distribution of potential market prices.
3. The specification of VAR in terms of a confidence interval; that is, that it provides the probability of the maximum the bank can afford to lose in a certain time frame, as set by senior bank management.

For example, assume a U.S. bank trade manager is holding in its portfolio a five-year $2,000,000 zero-coupon treasury note currently yielding 5.8 percent. The obvious risk this manager is facing is a rise in interest rates, which will undermine the market price of this position. What will be the bank's potential daily loss (VAR) should interest rates rise?

The answer to this question depends on three factors: the daily yield price sensitivity or volatility of the note; that is, its Modified Duration (MD), and the size of the adverse daily yield moves:

VAR = (–MD) (Adverse daily yield fluctuation) (Value of the position)[5]

Applying the MD formula discussed in the previous sections, the MD of this note can be calculated as follows:

$$MD = 1/1 + r = 5/1.058 = 4.726$$

Assuming further that the five-year treasury note yields follow a normal distribution, with an average of zero, and a standard deviation of 20 basis points (or 0.002) (see Figure 2.3);[6] and that bank management guidelines allow a 5-percent chance of exposure to adverse market conditions, there is a 2.5-percent chance that the note yield will fluctuate more than 39.2 basis points (1.96σ or 0.00392):

$$VAR = (–4.726) (0.00392) \$2,000,000 = \$37,051.84$$

This means that the bank takes a 2.5-percent chance that the note yield will fluctuate more than 3.92 basis points, and incur daily losses on this position reaching $37,051.84.

Figure 2.3
Five-Year Treasury Note Daily-Yield Distribution

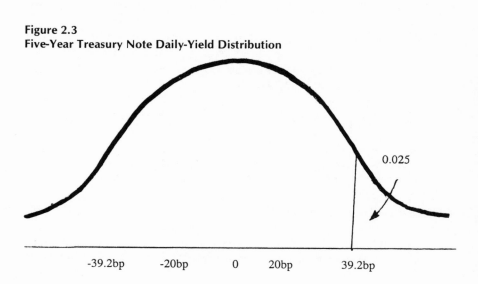

VAR works well for simple investment products, such as fixed income securities. As investment products proliferate and investment positions become more complicated, some experts have turned critical of this method. Professor Lo, for instance, argues that probabilities alone do not determine the risk exposure and hedging of a corporation: "Probabilities are an indispensable input into the risk-management process, but they do not determine how much risk a corporation should bear and how much should be hedged" (Lo 1998). Lo proposes an alternative method, Total Risk Management.

Total Risk Management

TRM takes into consideration the price paid for risk protection and investor's risk preference. "All three P's are central to TRM: prices in considering how much one must pay for hedging various risks; probabilities for assessing the likelihood of those risks; and preferences for deciding how much risk to bear and how much to hedge." Fong and Vasicek (1998) argue that "The complexities of the many risk factors and their interaction call for a multidimensional approach to risk management." Specifically, Fong and Vasicek propose a three-dimension risk measurement that includes sensitivity analysis and stress testing in addition to VAR (Treacy and Carey 1998, 1–27).

In short, banking risks are measured by both individual measures that measure the separate impact of each risk on bank performance, and aggregate measures that measure the comprehensive impact of all risks on bank's performance. Individual measures of interest rate risk include Duration, Gap Analysis, and Convexity. Individual measures of foreign exchange rate risk include FX Sensitivity or Gap Analysis. Individual measures of credit risk include Ratio Analysis, while individual investment risk measures include the Mean Variance Model, and the Capital Asset Pricing model. Aggregate risk measures include VAR and Total Risk Models.

In a fast-pace deregulated financial system, banking risk measurement is not a terminal, but an ongoing process. Financial risks must be continuously monitored and controlled.

Banking Risk Monitoring and Control

An integral part of the operational approach to risk management, banking monitoring and control begins with the formulation of policy objectives and guidelines, as determined by the philosophical approach toward risk adopted by senior management. Risk management guidelines specify the policy objectives of the bank and the aggregate risk it is willing to take to achieve these objectives. Aggressive banks, for instance, seeking higher returns for their depositors and stockholders, are willing to tolerate a higher level of risk. Conversely, conservative banks seeking moderate returns are willing to tolerate a lower level of risk.

In either case, risk management guidelines must set both aggregate and individual risk limits for close risk monitoring and control and are performed by newly established risk management departments, at the core of modern banking.

Risk Monitoring

As the term suggests, banking risk monitoring is the close following of banking risks by different levels of management to ensure that they remain within the tolerance limits, "red flags," set in the policy guidelines. As Timothy Haight (1997) puts it, "Careful monitoring of the bank's risks will provide management with the red flags whenever the risk levels are beyond those permitted as specified in the risk management guidelines" (p. 15).

To be effective, a risk monitoring system must be comprehensive; that is, it must follow all types and sources of risk. Interest rate risk monitoring systems, for instance, should monitor both position and income risks, on a consolidated basis to include the exposure to both the parent and the subsidiary companies. Likewise, foreign exchange risk monitoring systems should monitor the consolidated bank exposure to foreign exchange risk.

Risk monitoring requires a "risk-awareness" culture at all levels of management. It also requires both "hardware" and "software" technologies. Hardware technologies include high technology gear that provides the channels for the collection and the processing of risk information. Corporate intranet systems, for instance, allow the risk management department to share information with the trading desk and the credit department, and determine whether current assets and liabilities are in line with risk management guidelines. Bank intranets further allow senior management to share information with lower management, and determine at any moment whether the bank's risk exposure is consistent with certain policy objectives.

Software technologies include organizational structures and policies that enable bank managers to develop risk management skills. On-the-job and off-the-job training, for instance, provides bank managers the opportunity to learn and apply new risk management methods. Teamwork, job rotation, interdepartmental transfers, and bank-wide conferences allow bank managers to develop contextual knowledge of the bank business, and evaluate more accurately the various types of banking risks.

Software technologies further include the establishment of an internal system of checks and balances between the trading desk, the back office, the credit and the risk-management department, so as to improve risk control.

Risk Control

Risk control is about methods to lower or modify risks and contain them within the limits set forth in the risk management guidelines, and can be classified in two categories, on-balance sheet and off-balance sheet methods.

On-Balance Sheet Methods

On-balance sheet methods or Asset–Liability Management methods (ALM) focus on the restructuring of assets and liabilities, so as to minimize or even eliminate banking risks, especially the two traditional banking risks, liquidity and credit risk.

On-balance sheet risk management methods begin with the forecasting of major financial variables that may affect the bank performance, such as bank reserves, loan defaults, interest rates, foreign currency, and so on. Then, depending on the risk attitudes of bank management, it proceeds with the restructuring of assets and liabilities to ride on, avoid, mitigate, or take advantage of risks.

To control liquidity risk, for instance, conservative bank management can shorten the maturity of assets, and lengthen the maturity of liabilities, or combine the two. To shorten the maturity of its assets, management can add to its portfolio "self liquidating loans" or short-term government securities, such as two-year treasury notes. On-balance risk management methods include these:

Liquidity Risk	Credit Risk
"Self-liquidating loans"	Monitoring and forecasting of customer creditworthiness
Investment in T-bills	Termination clauses
Interbank borrowing	Collateral
High liquid securities	Diversification
Repurchase agreements (REPOs)	Securitization
Issuing bank bonds	Syndicated loans
Loan securitization	
Bankers acceptances	

To lengthen the maturity of its liabilities, management can issue longer maturity CDs. Ideally, a bank should immunize its portfolio against the liquidity by perfectly matching the maturity of its assets and liabilities.

Bank management can also control liquidity risk by developing good relations with other banks, institutional investors, and central bankers. Close relations with other banks, for instance, allow banks to quickly borrow funds in the interbank market. Close relations with institutional investors allow banks to securitize their loan portfolio and issue corporate bonds. Good relations with central bankers allow banks to turn to the borrowers of the "last resort," the discount window of central banks.

To control credit risk, bank management can restructure its balance sheet in three ways:

1. Diversify its asset portfolio to several industries and geographical locations, especially when those industries and locations display a negative correlation, for example, the oil vis-à-vis the transportation industries.
2. Resort to securitization of the loan portfolio, and loan syndication.
3. Screen carefully the creditworthiness of current and prospective clients, classifying them in different credit risk categories that determine risk premiums and collateral and other loan terms and conditions, an issue to be further addressed in Chapter 5.

To control interest risk, bank management must immunize its portfolio against interest rate fluctuations by matching interest-rate sensitive asset positions with interest-sensitive liabilities (interest rate income risk); and by matching the duration of its interest rate–sensitive assets with the duration of its interest rate–sensitive liabilities (position risk), an issue to be further addressed in Chapter 6. Likewise, to immunize the balance sheet against foreign currency risks, banks can match the foreign currency denominated assets with foreign currency denominated liabilities, an issue to be further addressed in Chapter 7.

Though simple and straightforward, on-balance sheet risk management has two major disadvantages. First, it is costly. Diversifying an investment portfolio, loading and unloading securities incurs transaction costs, and it may result in losses, especially when many large banks are trying to unload the same securities at the same time; it may further result in tax liabilities; and even violate certain bank policy objectives. Second, on-balance sheet management assumes inefficient financial markets, a not-so-realistic assumption in a global economy.

On-balance sheet risk management is inadequate, and often ineffective and inefficient in managing risks, especially interest rate and foreign exchange risks, and must be supplemented by off-balance sheet management.

Off-Balance Sheet Methods

As the term suggests, off-balance sheet methods are ways to lower banking risks by taking positions that do not appear on the balance sheet. Off-balance sheet risk-control methods apply financial derivative products, such as financial futures, options, and swaps to shift part or all of a banking risk to a third party, without altering portfolio positions. To shift credit risk to another party, for instance, banks can enter a credit swap or a credit option contract with a counterparty. To shift interest rate and foreign currency risks to another party, and foreign currency risks to third parties, banks can enter a broad array of interest rate and foreign currency derivatives contracts, which will be further addressed following the discussion of the evolution of banking risk management.

NOTES

1. Problems arising are related to classification in zones of certain asset and liability items. For example, it is difficult to classify demand deposits, because withdrawal time is not known, so many bank managers classify them in the overnight zone. Yet as it is statistically estimated, not all the depositors ask for their deposits at the same time, so a better choice is to classify a portion of such deposits to several zones; and a similar policy should apply regarding revolving credit.

2. A "short position" is the obligation to buy a liability. Examples of on-balance sheet short positions are customer deposits, other financial institutions deposits, repurchase agreements, spot transactions of foreign exchange against domestic currency, spot transactions of a foreign currency against another foreign currency, and so on. Examples of off-balance sheet short positions are swap obligations (future flow), forward outright, Letter of credit, interest rate instruments, and so on. A long position is the obligation to buy an asset. Examples of on-balance sheet long positions are short-term and long-term loans, investments in bonds (treasury or private), and in stock. Examples for off-balance sheet long positions are obligations from swaps (future flow) or forward outright, letters of credit, and so on.

3. Markowitz 1999, 4.

4. Ibid., 253.

5. Known as "Metrics," this approach was first developed by J. P. Morgan in 1994.

6. Probability distributions can be estimated either from historical data or simulations.

3

Evolution of Banking
Risk Management

In banking, we used to have a fairly simple business model:
Find loans; structure them, administer, and collect; and fund
them with deposits.
            Rolling Meadows and Norman McClave (1996, 29)

No organization is immune to risk. Moreover, each organization's risks change constantly. While reaction is sometimes necessary, detecting and reacting are insufficient as ways of
managing risk. Every organization must learn to anticipate and
prevent by implementing effective processes throughout the
company so that it proactively identifies, measures, and controls business risk.
                                    A. Andersen (1995, 2)

As is the case with management in general, banking risk management is an ever-changing process shaped by general factors, such
as the institution objectives, financial trends, and government regulation; and by special factors, such as the structure and cost of liabilities, the structure and returns of assets, the maturity structure
of assets and liabilities, and the size and source of the risk assumed
by each asset and liability item.

Banking risk management adopts and adapts to the evolution and the revolution in the industry structure and environment. In the first three-quarters of the twentieth century, a period known as "multinationalization," banking risk management was an "on-balance sheet" operation, handed by treasury and finance departments, and focusing on the two traditional banking risks, the liquidity risk and the credit risk (see Table 3.1).[1] In the last quarter of the century, a period known as "globalization," banks continued to manage liquidity and credit risks, but their focus shifted to two new risks, the foreign exchange and the interest rate risks (see Table 3.1).

Addressing the evolution of risk management in the twentieth century, this chapter is in two sections. The first section reviews the banking environment, industry structure, and risk management under multinationalization. The second section reviews the banking environment, industry structure, and risk management under globalization.

BANKING RISK MANAGEMENT
UNDER MULTINATIONALIZATION

As briefly discussed in the previous chapters, for several decades after the beginning of the First World War, the world commodity market was a fragmented, a moribund market, consisting of a collection of separate national and local markets. Market fragmentation, in turn, and long-term relations between manufacturers, suppliers, distributors, and retailers provided a sanctuary, a low-risk environment for local corporations, including the subsidiaries of multinational corporations. Tariffs, quotas, and diverse product standards limited competition across national markets, while government regulation and long-term relations limited competition across local markets. Currency controls limited currency fluctuations and the unfavorable effects on cross-border corporate financial flows (transaction risk) and asset transfer (translation risk), especially the case for multinational corporations, which frequently transfer financial flows and assets between headquarters and subsidiaries around the world. Interest rate controls limited interest rate fluctuations and their own unfavorable effect on corporate financial flows and sources of financing, especially for highly leveraged industries.

Market fragmentation and long-term relations were not limited to commodity markets, they extended to financial markets, also a collection of disjointed segments, banking, securities, and insurance. Market fragmentation limited interindustry and intraindustry

Table 3.1
Evolution of Banking Risks in the Twentieth Century

Period	Focus on	Method
Multinationalization	Traditional risks	On-balance sheet
(1900–1975)	Liquidity	
	Credit	
Globalization	Nontraditional risks	On and off-balance sheet
(1976–present)	Interest rate	
	Foreign exchange	

competition, providing a sanctuary for each industry segment and most notably banking, which has been tightly regulated by finance departments, central banks, and antitrust agencies, especially after the early 1930s. Central banks, for instance, set reserve requirements, and interest rate and credit ceilings. Antitrust agencies limited bank mergers, acquisitions, and industry concentration. Treasury departments and ministries of finance protected the industry from competition from other financial sectors, namely from the securities and the insurance industries. "Nearly every facet of banking activity is regulated by federal and state banking law. The maximum amount of credit extended to one borrower is regulated as are the total amounts of some loans. The investment portfolio of banks must meet certain standards. The amount of reserves that a bank must maintain is determined by law and/or by government agencies" (Reed 1963, 30). In the United States for instance, the Glass–Steagall Act or Banking Act of 1933 raised a "wall" between banking and the rest of the service industry; authorized the Federal Reserve Bank (FED) to impose interest rate ceilings (Regulation Q); and established the Federal Deposit Insurance Corporation (FDIC). The McFadden Act of 1927 prohibited cross-state branching without host state permission. The Bank Holding Company Act of 1956 defined the activities of banking holding companies, while a host of consumer protection and transparency acts of the 1970s defined the parameters of consumer bank lending.

Selective U.S. Banking Regulations

The National Currency Act of 1863 and the National Banking Act of 1864
- Reinforced by subsequent legislation, the two acts prohibited banks from owning stocks

New York State Insurance Legislation (1906)
- Separated insurance from investment banking and the dealing in corporate bonds and stocks

The Glass–Steagall Act (1933)
- Separated banking from the rest of the financial service industry, especially the insurance and securities services
- Authorized the Federal Reserve to impose deposit interest rate ceilings on banks and thrift institutions (Regulation Q)
- Established Federal Deposit Insurance Corporation

The McFadden Act (1927)
- Prohibited banks from branching across state lines without permission from the host state

The Banking Act of 1935
- It expanded the power of the Federal Reserve to set reserve requirements and to control long-term deposit interest rates

The Bank Holding Company Act and the Douglas Amendment (1956)
- It defined a bank holding company as one that holds at least 25 percent of the voting stock in two or more banks
- It defined the activities of bank holding companies, prohibiting new acquisitions outside their home state, in essence protecting local banks
- Initiated the separation of banking from commerce; that is, it prohibited banks from owning voting shares in nonbank companies

Banking Merger Act of 1960; and the Bank Holding Act Amendments (1966)
- Federal agencies must approve mergers and holding companies' expansion

Amendment of the Banking Holding Act (1970)
- Equity investing is allowed only after the Federal Reserve Board approval and should be "passive"

Consumer Protection/Transparency Acts of 1970s (Regulation Z)
- Fair Credit Reports Act
- Fair Debt Collection Act
- Equal Credit Opportunity Act
- Community Reinvestment Act
- The Bank Secrecy Act
- The Right to Privacy Act

International Banking Act (1978)
- Placed foreign banks in the United States under federal supervision

Basle Accord of 1988
- Established risk-adjusted international capital requirements for banks and other financial institutions

In Europe, regulators didn't reach as far as the United States in separating banking from the rest of the financial service industry. In Germany, for instance, Hausenbanks served as universal banks, providing a broad array of services, including the underwriting of securities, the selling of insurance through subsidiaries, and even investing in equity and real estate. Banks further took direct equity positions in companies, tightening up their performance to that of their corporate clients. In Belgium, banks have been permitted to enter the securities industry directly or through subsidiaries, and the insurance industry through subsidiaries only, while in Greece, banks have been permitted to pursue securities underwriting.

European governments directly owned banking institutions, controlled interest rates, and rationed credit to finance government deficits and targeted industries. In Spain, for instance, regional governments owned savings banks (*cajas*). In 1945, in England, the Committee of London Clearing Bankers (CLCB) determined that demand deposits with a balance less than 2,500 pounds should bear no interest, while demand deposits in excess of that balance should earn an interest of one-and-a-half percent. CLCB further required a fourteen-day deposit withdrawal notice; and set the rules for overdraft accounts. In 1945, in France, Conseil National du Credit (CNC) set interest-rate ceilings on demand deposits and interest rate floors on loans. CNC was further empowered to liquidate or merge banks. In Greece, the Bank of Greece mandated that 40 percent of bank deposits should be allotted to the purchase of treasury bills, 11 percent for the financing of small and medium enterprises, and 1 percent for the financing of public utilities.

In Japan, the powerful Ministry of Finance (MOF) and the Ministry of Trade and Industry (MITI), in essence, rationed credit to a number of industries targeted for development at the time. MOF regulation insulated banks from outside competition, while preventing excessive competition within the industry. Exchange rate controls and restrictions on foreign capital flows limited the entry of foreign banks and securities companies into the Japanese financial markets, eliminating foreign currency risks. The Securities and Exchange Law of 1948, the Japanese version of the Glass–Steagall Act of 1933, limited competition between traditional banking and securities, except for the purchase of securities for their own accounts. Financial regulation further segmented the banking industry into city banks, regional banks, and trust banks, overseeing their day-to-day operations, and protected the industry from both internal and external competition. Thus, Japan's tight banking regulation replicates a government cartel, a *Gosou Sendan Houshiki*, an "Escorted Convoy System." MOF "destroyers" protect banks from outsiders and ensure that they are all moved in tandem, without crushing each other (see Figure 3.1).

Supplementing tight government regulation, long term relations between banks and their corporate clients further limited competition and the traditional banking risks associated with it. Close relations between banks and their corporate clients provided bank managers firsthand information about their clients' economic and financial situation and prospects, so they could intuitively evaluate and assess credit risks. This was especially true with large corporate clients, the primary recipients of bank credit. As Michael Milken (1999) puts it: "Back in the 1960s, a small number of money-center banks and large insurance companies pretty much determined who got access to U.S. financial capital. Their customers were large, established corporations—companies with history—and capital was allocated to these 800 or so 'investment grade' firms based on a look in the rear-view mirror" (p. A8).

Firsthand information and long experience in an industry, which is "essentially a business of information," in the words of Peter Bakstansky, vice president of the Federal Reserve Bank of New York, provided banks an advantage over potential competitors from other segments of the finance industry. As Martin Mayer puts it, "Once upon a time a network of information providers was required for a lender to learn the panoply of market interest rates at different maturity dates, foreign-exchange rates, credit worthiness of importunate borrowers, and so forth. Only a bank, which could spread the costs of gathering information over a variety of customers and transactions, could maintain the necessary, constantly changing

Figure 3.1
Gosou Sendan Houshiki

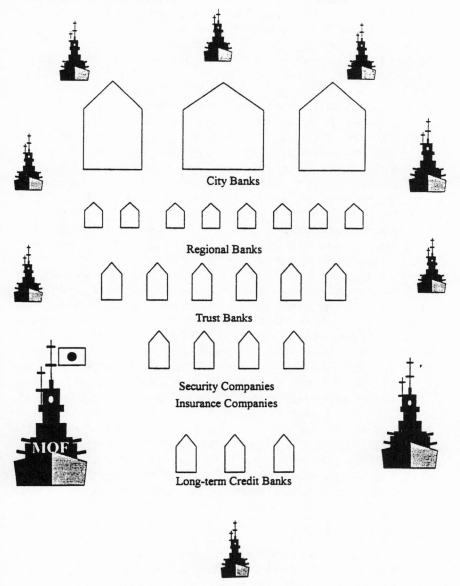

City Banks

Regional Banks

Trust Banks

Security Companies
Insurance Companies

Long-term Credit Banks

Source: From *The Rise and Fall of Abacus Banking in Japan and China*, Yuko Arayama and Panos Mourdoukoutas, p. 48, Copyright © 2000 by Yuko Arayama and Panos Mourdoukoutas. Reproduced with permission of Greenwood Publishing Group, Inc., Westport, CT.

library of facts and figures" (Milken 1999, A8). In this sense, banks were the "hub" of every transaction: "If banks are the door to information, we control the menu. We are not merely the repository for cash, but instead are the hub from which all transactions begin" (Randle 1995, 47).

In addition to accommodating the collection of firsthand information, close relations between banks and central bankers and their corporate clients spread risks, especially for "syndicated" loans. This was especially true in Asia and most notably in Japan where business-to-business relations and relations between banks and their clients often supported by long-lasting cross-ownership holdings are the important factors in evaluating prospective clients and in extending credit to them.[2] In 1988, banks held 17 percent of the Tokyo Stock Exchange–listed shares, while corporations held 44 percent of the bank-listed shares (Stock Sales Cut into Cross-Holdings 1998, 11).

Information inefficiencies, government protection and regulation, and long-term bank relations made banking a low-risk business, and risk management a minor factor in bank management. "The presence of regulation impacts on risk in at least two ways: first, it may regulate risk taking itself; and, secondly, the risk taking activity may, to varying degrees be underwritten by the financial system at large reducing the requirement for risk management in individual organizations" (Das 1997, 548). Banking was confined to the "agglomeration of the transaction balances of the community to lend at interest its commercial enterprise," as Adam Smith would have put it, a function that in the United States and Japan is reflected in the steady rise of the asset accumulation/financial intermediation ratio (see Figure 3.2).

Narrow interest rate and foreign currency fluctuations and little competition from the other segments of the financial service industry resulted in a dual strategy toward financial risks, a passive, "do nothing" strategy toward interest rate and foreign exchange risks, and an active strategy toward liquidity and credit risks.

Liquidity-Risk Management

In the first three decades of the century, a period in which banks drew almost all of their liabilities from demand deposits, liquidity risk management was confined to the asset side of the balance sheet, and the loan portfolio in particular. Bankers monitored closely the maturity of the loan portfolio, and the flow of loan repayments, especially "self-liquidating" loans or real bills, loans that matured

Figure 3.2
Asset Accumulation and Financial Intermediation in Japan and the United States (1954–1988)

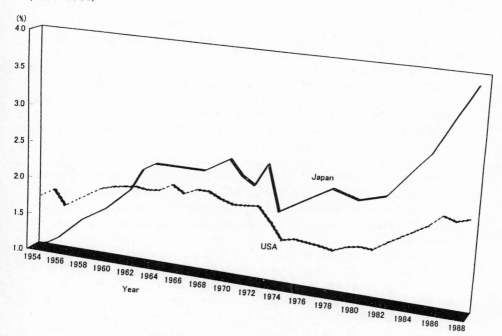

Source: OECD, *Economic Surveys, Japan 1990/1991* (Paris: OECD, 1992), p. 77.

as soon as the underlying collateral, merchandise in production or transit, was delivered, providing a steady source of liquidity.

Historically, liquidity management focused on assets and was closely tied to lending policies. Under the *commercial loan theory* prior to 1930, banks were encouraged to make only short-term, self-liquidating loans. Such loans closely matched the maturity of bank deposits and enabled banks to meet deposit withdrawals with funds from maturing loans. An inventory loan, for example, would be paid when the borrower sold the items that coincided with the need for financing to accumulate additional inventory. A bank was liquid if its loan portfolio consisted of short-term loans. (Koch 1988, 276)

For the next three decades of the century (1930–1960), liquidity-risk management continued on the asset side of the balance sheet, but the focus shifted from the loan portfolio to the investment portfolio, for two reasons. First, the combination of a sluggish demand for loans and a conservative credit policy on the part of banks in the aftermath of the Great Depression and the massive bank failures associated with it reduced opportunities in this area. Second, the introduction of treasury bills in 1929 and the government issued and government guaranteed securities in the mid-1930s provided an alternative, low-risk investment. To improve liquidity, for instance, banks invested in staggered-maturity treasury bills and other government securities. Reflecting this shift, in 1950, for instance, close to 50 percent of bank investment portfolios was allocated to federal, state, and local government securities (Cooper and Fraser 1984).

In the next fifteen years (1960–1975), as banks came up with new methods to shorten loan portfolio maturity and amass deposits, risk management expanded to both sides of the balance sheet, and therefore became known as "asset liability management." "Available liquidity sources are identified and compared to expected needs by a bank's asset and liability management committee (ALCO). Management considers all potential deposit outflows and inflows when deciding how to allocate assets and finance operations" (Koch 1988, 278).

To expand liquidity of bank portfolio on the asset side of the bank balance sheet, for instance, banks resorted to securitization, the bundling together of fixed-rate mortgages and then selling them to investors:

Securitization can reduce various risks of the direct lenders. Lenders can sell their loans in securitized form and buy the loans of other packaged securities. This can provide geographic diversity and reduce business-line concentrations in loan portfolios and eliminate the need for lenders to hold loans to a single borrower. In addition, selling loans can reduce the risk that banks bear when interest rates change the value of the loans they are holding. (Feldman 1995, 23–30)

To expand liquidity on the liability side, banks issued commercial paper in the Eurodollar market developed in the 1960s. Banks also issued long-term savings and large CDs lengthening the maturity; and they would extend loan commitments first, and then raise the required funds by selling CDs.

In the United States the development of competitive bidding for large scale deposits is associated with the negotiable certificate of deposit (CD). Such certificates, first issued in 1961, grew rapidly in importance. Subsequently CDs spread to a number of other countries and are now traded in markets parallel to those in large time deposits. Other instruments with varying degrees of negotiability have become of importance in other countries. (OECD 1987, 41)

Reflecting this restructuring in bank liabilities, time deposits increased from around 25 percent of bank liabilities in 1950 to around 52 percent by 1975. Certificates of deposit rose from a few million when introduced in 1961 to close to 200 billion by 1975, while demand deposits increased from $100 to $250 billion over the same period (OECD 1987, 41).

In all three periods, banks closely monitored relations with central bankers and other banks. Close relations with other banks and central bankers, for instance, allowed banks to borrow in the interbank market and the Overnight Repurchase Agreement (Repos) market, boosting liquidity. Close relations with central banks allowed banks, and the banking industry as a whole to borrow from the discount window, further boosting liquidity and seigniorage income. This was especially true in countries that viewed monetary policy as a tool to promote rapid economic growth like Japan's (Arayama and Mourdoukoutas 2000).

Known as "over-borrowing" or "over-lending," this policy of over-lending can be traced back to the turn of the century, as a vehicle of financing the country's industrialization. "In expanding their loan business, the most powerful banks were able to borrow at special rates from the Bank of Japan, while smaller banks borrowed from the major banks. Through borrowing from the Bank of Japan, the commercial banks were enabled to make loans to industrial enterprises at levels well above those permitted by their own liabilities"

(Lazonick and O'Sullivan 1997, 120). Thus, the policy "chronically extended more credit, either by lending or by purchase of securities, than they acquired from deposits or own capital. The gap was filled primarily by relying on borrowings from the Bank of Japan" (Suzuki 1987, 22).

In short, in the first three-quarters of the twentieth century, conventional liquidity risk management underwent several stages, shifting focus back and forth from the loan to the investment portfolio, and eventually extending to both sides of the balance sheet; and relying on the close ties between bank managers and corporate clients, as well as close ties with other banks, and government regulators.

Credit-Risk Management

As was the case with conventional liquidity risk management, in the first quarter of the twentieth century, the focus of credit-risk management was on the loan portfolio, for two reasons. First, robust economic growth fuelled demand for corporate loans. Second, the retirement of U.S. government debt made investments in U.S. government securities a limited alternative. Indeed, during the period 1900–1925, roughly 70 percent of all commercial bank deposits were allocated to loans (Reed 1963, 162).

For the period 1925–1955, the focus of credit-risk management shifted to the investment portfolio, for two reasons. First, the U.S. economy slowed down substantially, curtailing the demand for loans. Second, the acceleration of the U.S. government deficits, and the issuance of instruments such as treasury bills, treasury bonds, Government National Mortgage Associations offered banks a low risk alternative. Indeed, during the period 1926–1950, investments increased from about 28 to 60 percent of all commercial bank deposits (Reed 1963, 162).

For the period 1960–1975, as the U.S. economy picked up steam, boosting loan demand, credit-risk management shifted back to the loan portfolio, and the diversification to mortgages and consumer loans. Indeed, for the period 1950–1975, the investment–deposit ratio dropped from 60 percent down to 30 percent, while the loan–deposit ratio increased from around 25 percent in 1950 to around 50 percent (Reed 1963, 162).

As was the case with liquidity-risk management, in all periods, credit-risk management emphasized relational banking, that is, the nurturing of close relations between professional lending officers and bank clients. "The customer relationship develops between the bank and those good borrowers who borrow regularly. Therefore, a borrower that becomes a steady customer will bring more loan demand to the bank in the future than in the past. As interest rates rise, future loan demand and the steady loan demand of good customers become more important to the bank" (Mason 1979, 86).

Close customer relations, in turn, allowed credit officers to monitor and measure customer performance and creditworthiness of their clients, especially before 1930s when banking catered to the local community. As Mayer (1997) puts it: "The real banker was the lending officer, and it was the lending officer who became Chairman and CEO of the bank. He knew his borrowers business. Before the 1930s, the expertise was almost always a matter of geography: banks lent in their own baliwick" (p. 198). Specifically, close monitoring and measuring customer performance further allowed credit managers to develop scoring techniques that ranked customers according to the probability to repay their loans; and set risk premiums, collateral, and other loan conditions that hedge the bank's position, an issue to be further addressed in Chapter 5.

Close customer relations and accounting and business relations were accommodated by robust economic growth, which boosted deposits and loan demand allowing banks to compete on loan volume. A steady loan volume, in turn, was followed by a steady flow of earnings. In the United States, for instance, between 1935 and 1975 commercial banks' annual returns on assets remained steady, between 0.6 and 0.8 percent. Annual rates of returns climbed, from around 2 percent in 1965 to 12 percent in 1980, while bank failures remained isolated events (Waldrop 1999, 47).

In short, for about three-quarters of the century, bank management adopted a dual strategy toward financial risks, a passive, a "do nothing" strategy toward interest and exchange rate risks, and an active strategy toward liquidity and credit risks. Banking was more of a routine accounting and human-relations management function and less of a risk-management operation, a function that was to change under globalization.

BANKING RISK MANAGEMENT UNDER GLOBALIZATION

Since the mid-1970s, the increasing integration of national and local markets brought about by the resumption of globalization in the late 1970s has eliminated market sanctuaries. Driven by the collapse of communist and fascist regimes, the establishment of the World Trade Organization (WTO), the expansion and strengthening of regional organizations, the weakening of unions, deregulation and privatization, and the spread of information technology, globalization has been a mixed blessing for businesses. On the bright side, globalization has been a source of efficiency and opportunity, expanding sales and raising profits. The creation of the WTO and the lifting of protectionism, for instance, allowed companies to expand their presence around the world with the same ease as in their local market, attaining economies of scale and saving billions of dollars in tariffs and bureaucratic customs procedures. The weakening of unions allowed companies a higher degree of flexibility in adjusting the quantity and quality of its labor inputs to changing economic and technological conditions. The collapse of socialism expanded business horizons to former socialist countries of Eastern Europe, the former Soviet Republics, and Asia, while deregulation and privatization opened up several economic sectors to private enterprises. The spread of information technology allowed companies to communicate efficiently and effectively, reduce inventories, find new ways to market, distribute their products and convey their services to customers.

On the dark side, globalization is a source of compounding uncertainty manifested in excessive competition and productive capacity, rising risks, price and business destruction, and lower profit margins. This is especially true for companies in industries that are at the forefront of globalization, such as automobiles, telecommunications, semiconductors, computers, and consumer electronics, where excess capacity has been driving prices sharply lower. In some industries, such as in investing and retailing, globalization and information technology allow buyers and suppliers to communicate directly and momentarily with each other, eliminating the information vacuum that often gave advantage to one supplier over another. A computer and a modem are all buyers need to visit virtual markets around the globe and execute transactions with just a simple keyboard stroke.

Globalization and its impact extends to service markets and most notably to finance, which is being transformed from a collection of disjointed segments to a single integrated sector. "The traditional lines separating banking from other financial services activities have been increasingly blurred as banks and thrifts offer new financial products and as more nonfinancial firms enter into the banking business through ownership of limited-service bank charters and unitary thrifts" (Waldrop 1999, 47).

The 1997 WTO Financial Agreement, for instance, has leveled the field in global financial markets, providing new opportunities for financial firms and banks. In the United States, the Depository

Institutions Deregulation and Monetary Act of 1980 (DIDMA) introduced Super Now accounts and subjected all deposits in credit institutions to the reserve requirement rule. The Garn–St. Germain Depository Institutions Act of 1982 lifted Regulation Q, fostering competition between thrifts and commercial banks for deposits, and the Riegle–Neal Interstate Banking and Branching Efficiency Act of 1994 superseded the Douglas Amendment, and the McFadden Act had removed major barriers to cross-state acquisitions by bank holding companies, paving the way for interstate banking and creating new business.

Selective Financial Deregulation Legislation in the United States and the WTO

The International Banking Act of 1978

- Created a fair competitive environment between U.S. banks and the branches of foreign banks

The Depository Institutions Deregulation and Monetary Act of 1980 (DIDMA)

- Allowed the introduction of Super Now accounts and subjected all deposits in credit institutions to reserve requirement rule

The Garn–St. Germain Act of 1982

- Lifted Regulation Q (eliminated interest rate ceilings), which allowed thrifts and commercial banks to compete for deposits
- Allowed the introduction of new financial products, such as money market and Super Now accounts

Riegle–Neal Interstate Banking and Branching Efficiency Act of 1994

- Eliminated most federal restrictions on interstate banking. Thus, bank holding companies with multiple subsidiary banks in several states could consolidate affiliates into one bank with branches outside its home state
- Allowed savings and loans associations to make commercial loans
- Limited deposit concentrations in any one bank to 30 percent of a state's deposits, and 10 percent of the nation's deposits
- Revised Regulation K
- Expanded the overseas powers of the U.S. banks

Gramm and Leach Act (1999)

- Allowed the direct affiliation among U.S. banks, securities, and insurance companies

- Created "financial superstores," like the one created after the merger of Citigroup and Travelers

WTO Financial Agreement of 1997
- Leveled the field in global financial markets
- Provided new global opportunities for financial firms

In Europe, a host of EU directives that followed the Basle Committee recommendations have laid the foundation for free EU banking and the management of market risks. To branch across member states, banking institutions must meet certain capital and reserve requirements, and comply with the laws and regulations of the other institutions of the host states. Advancing the objective of free banking, Directive 89/646 and Directive 93/22 provided the foundation for the creation of the single licensing by deregulating the financial products and services that banks and other financial institutions in the European Union could offer, irrespective of the country licensed. Directive 93/6 set common capital adequacy supervision and control of banks to protect customers.

EU directives were supplemented by deregulation measures taken by member states. Great Britain, for instance, ended the "collective agreements," among clearing bankers, and eliminated interest rate deposit and loan controls (Reed 1963, 77). Germany created the *Allfinanz*, universal banks, institutions that accept deposits and offer almost every financial product, from loans to life insurance and mutual funds.

Selective Basle Committee Rules and Corresponding European Union Directives

Basle Committee	European Union
Capital Accord (1988) It is expected to be revised and include market risk in the loan portfolio.	Directive 89/647 (capital solvency ratio) and Directive 89/299 (definition of bank's own capital)
Amendment of the previous (Capital Accord) directive for the inclusion of provisions and loan loss reserves ratios (1991)	Directive 91/633
Amendment to the Capital Accord to incorporate market risk (1996, Part a)	Amendment of capital adequacy directive with Directives 93/22 and 93/6
Credit-risk rules of certain off-balance sheet items (1994) and the potential exposure for off-balance sheet items (1995)	Directive 96/10

Amendment to the Capital Accord
to incorporate market risk (1996,
Part b) modification of the market
risk amendment (1997)

Capital adequacy Directive 93/6
modification

Japan, under what is known as the "Big Bang," disbanded the "Escorted Convoy System" and the cozy environment it had provided for the banking industry (see Figure 3.3). Interest rates on demand and time deposits have been fully liberalized; Foreign Exchange and Foreign Trade Law took effect, liberalizing cross-border transactions; commissions on stock transactions in excess of 50 million yen were deregulated; investment trusts were created; financial disclosure rules were strengthened; and there was improvement in the diversity and efficiency of financial markets.

The transformation of the financial service industry from a collection of disjointed segments to a single integrated industry has been a source of opportunity for the banking industry. The lowering of domestic and international market barriers has allowed banks to pursue business in other local and international markets. The lowering of entry barriers to the rest of the financial industry and the liberalization of interest rates has expanded opportunities in the asset management and insurance segment of the financial service industries. The spread of information technology has allowed banks to develop less expensive self-service delivery channels. "More banks are adopting home-banking transaction capabilities via the World Wide Web, sometimes even in favor of PC-based approaches" (Kolor 1996, 1). According to a survey by the consulting firm Booz, Allen, and Hamilton, over 16 million customers made use of the internet for their banking needs (Kolor 1996, 1). Another survey by the same consulting firm finds that information technology has lowered the average cost of a bank transaction from $1.07 to 0.54, ATM machines lowered it to 0.27, PC banking to 0.15, and the internet to 0.10 (Costanzo 1997, 1).

Banks are turning into both actual and virtual one-stop financial shops selling almost every financial product, mutual funds, stocks, and insurance, deriving a substantial part of their revenues from fees rather than from interest income. Reflecting this "commoditization" of banking, for the period 1984–1997, noninterest income increased from 25 percent to 38 percent of bank net operating revenue (Costanzo 1997, 47). Major banks, such as J. P. Morgan earn more of their income from investment fees than from financial intermediation.

The transformation of the finance industry has also been a source of risks and uncertainties for banks, as manifested in three trends.

Figure 3.3
The Disbanding of Gosou Sendan Houshiki

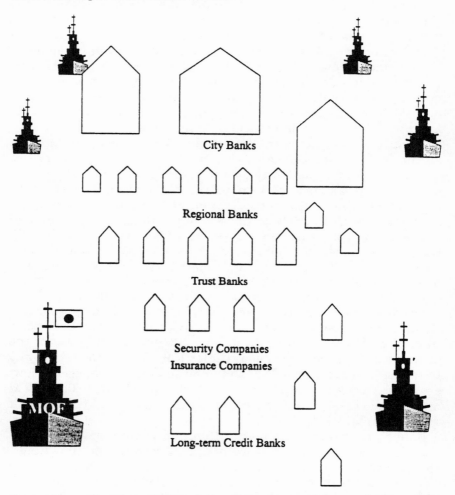

City Banks

Regional Banks

Trust Banks

Security Companies
Insurance Companies

Long-term Credit Banks

First, the expansion of banks to the emerging economies of the former socialist countries and the Asian and Latin American developing economies has magnified traditional credit and liquidity risk. The Asian crisis of 1997 and the Russian debt moratorium of 1998 attest to it. Globalization has also magnified a nontraditional risk, the interest-rate risk, as reflected in the standard deviation of the ten-year T-bond, which increased from 0.72 in the 1/77–9/79 period to 1.62 in the 1/85–12/86 period (Koch 1988, 11).

Second, as Cooper and Fraser (1984) pointed out two decades ago, "Financial innovations developed in recent periods may have permanently reduced the market share of depository financial institutions. The direct evidence relates to the enormous expansion in financial services offered by non-depository financial institutions" (p. 4). As Cumming (1998) puts it, "Competition in the financial market has increased dramatically with the globalization of financial activity, the rapid pace of financial innovation and the reshaping of financial services by advances in information technology. The force of international competition during the past two decades has flattened the distinctions between banking and securities activities, and, increasingly, between these and insurance activities" (p. 21).

Competition does not come just from domestic, but from distant competitors, too. As Badger (1995) puts it, "Isolated economies no longer exist. We moved to one financial market a long time ago: the whole world. Competition is fierce. Rivalry comes not only from the bank down the street or around the corner but from other sources and from around the world" (p. 32). This is a trend that is expected to continue in the near future, as banks will be losing their conventional information advantage.

The nature of competition in retail banking, and in retail financial services more generally, could be radically changed by the movement to electronics. Consumers will have access to more information, from more competitors, in a faster time, than ever before. Banks, nonbank providers of financial services, and technology companies will all, at least to some extent, be trying to establish the primary relationship with the consumer, while in some cases providing services to one another or perhaps even selling each other products. (Patrikis 1997, 7)

In the United States, "There is other direct evidence that the financial innovations developed in recent periods may have permanently reduced the market share of depository institutions. The direct evidence relates to the enormous expansion in financial service offered by nondepository financial institutions. The direct evidence relates to the differences in the burden of regulation for nondepository as compared to depository financial institutions" (Cooper and Fraser 1984, 4). According to data compiled by Ernst and Young and the American Bankers Association for the period 1974–1994, banks lost almost one-third of their deposits to nonbank financial institutions, such as insurance companies, pension funds, mutual funds and money market funds, even traditional nonfinancial firms (Cohen 1996, 1). The share of total credit provided by the banking industry has declined from 40.1 percent in 1950 to 32 percent by 1982. Over the same period, the share of government bonds in bank portfolio has decreased from 43 percent to 14 percent, while mortgages have increased from 9 percent to 20 percent, and consumer credit from 5 percent to 13 percent. According to U.S. Federal Reserve Bank data, mutual fund assets increased from $135 billion in 1980 to over $2,824 billion in 1995. Total outstanding commercial paper increased from $124 billion in 1980 to $675 billion in 1995. Annual junk-bond debt increased from $36 billion in 1980 to $445 billion in 1995. The value of U.S.–backed securities underwriting increased from $8 billion in 1983 to $479 billion in 1993. Annual eurobond issues have increased from $44 billion in 1983 to $344 billion by 1995.

Third, banks have been losing their "core" low-risk large corporate clients, which now can raise capital directly in equity markets. "The spread of information technology and the dramatic advances in financial theory have made it cheaper for big companies to raise money in the capital markets rather [than] from the banks" (*The Economist* 1999, 4). This, in turn, pushed banks to extend lending to small and medium enterprises, lowering the quality of loans. "Since 1993, the credit quality of banks' portfolios has declined sharply. The better-rated companies increasingly raise money from capital markets" ("On a Wing and a Prayer" 1999, 7). This was especially true in Japan in the late 1980s, when deregulation allowed large companies to draw funds directly from the equity and debt markets.

In short, in the last quarter of the century, globalization, government deregulation, and information efficiencies have made banking a high-risk business, and risk management a major factor in bank management. Globalization and the forces that support and reenforce it have left banks vulnerable to highly volatile financial markets, which can result in windfall of gains or losses in the bank's performance. Banking is no longer confined to the "agglomeration of transaction balances of the community," but extends to both on-balance sheet and off-balance sheet risk management to achieve certain risk-rewards objectives. Thus, one of the most pressing issues banks are confronted with is the management of risks associated with bank earnings.

Initially, risk management continued to be an on balance sheet operation, but its focus shifted to the two financial market risks, the interest rate and the foreign exchange risks. Bankers forecasted interest rates and the foreign exchange rates and portfolio immunization; that is, the rearrangement of bank portfolio to take advantage of anticipated interest and foreign exchange moves. In periods of rising interest rates, banks assigned floating rate loans, invested in floating income securities, and issued long-term maturity CDs. Conversely, in periods of falling interest rates, banks assigned fixed interest rate loans, invested in fixed rate securities, and issued short-term CDs.

As discussed in Chapter 2, portfolio immunization ran into a number of problems and most notably to the failure of bankers to accurately and consistently predict the direction of interest rates and foreign exchange rates. Often banks run losses that eroded their performance and resulted in the crisis of the 1980s.

Addressing these problems, banks applied financial derivatives to hedge their balance sheet against interest rate and foreign exchange fluctuations. In the 1970s, for instance, banks turned to foreign currency futures to hedge foreign exchange risks and to treasury bond futures to hedge interest rate risk. In the 1980s, banks broadened their choice of foreign exchange and interest rate hedging instruments to include foreign exchange and interest rate swaps, eurodollar options, and swaptions.

The introduction of selective risk management tools is as follows:

1970s
- Foreign currency forward contracts
- Foreign currency futures
- Equity options
- T-bond futures

1980s
- Currency swaps
- Interest rate swaps; T-note futures; equity index; Eurodollar futures
- Eurodollar options; swaptions
- Equity index swaps
- Credit default options

To sum up, banking risk management has been an ever-changing process, adopting and adapting to changes in the market environment and industry structure. In the first three-quarters of the twentieth century, banking risk management was an on-balance sheet operation, focusing on the two traditional risks, liquidity and credit risk. Liquidity risk was managed with sound accounting, by shortening the maturity of assets and by extending the maturity of liabilities, and by maintaining close relations with other banks and central bankers. Credit risk was managed by relational banking; that is, the cultivation of close ties with customers that allowed banks to closely monitor and measure their customers' creditworthiness.

In the last quarter of the twentieth century, banking risk management was extended and supplemented by off-balance sheet operation, focusing on interest rate and foreign exchange risk with the use of financial derivatives, an issue to be further addressed after a brief description of financial derivatives.

NOTES

1. For a detailed discussion of multinationalization and globalization, see Mourdoukoutas (1999, ch. 2).

2. In this sense, Japan's banking system is similar to that of Germany where banks are allowed to hold equity positions and are active in corporate governance.

4

Risk Management Methods:
Financial Derivatives

> Derivatives, structured notes, and other complex financial instruments fulfil important functions in the financial marketplace. Used properly, these products can effectively reduce risks and provide stability. When used responsibly, derivatives can also be used to increase investment returns.
>
> Senator Alfonse M. D'Amato (1995, 1)

As discussed in the previous chapters, the proliferation of financial risks that followed globalization has fuelled financial reengineering, the development of financial derivatives, products that allow banks and investors in general to hedge financial risks; that is, shift them to third parties.

The development of interest rate derivatives, such as Forward Rate Agreements (FRAs), Interest Rate Futures (IRFs), interest rate futures options, interest rate caps, floors and collars, and interest rate swaps, allow banks to shift interest rate risks to third parties. The development of foreign currency derivatives, such as Forward Exchange Rate Contracts (FERC), foreign currency futures and options, and foreign currency swaps allow banks to hedge their positions against foreign exchange risks, while credit derivatives allow banks to hedge credit risk.

As of June 1998, interest rate derivatives dominated the OTC derivatives market reaching a notional amount of $24,124 billion and a gross market value of $1,354 billion, followed by foreign exchange derivatives of a notional amount of $22,055 billion and a gross market value of $982 billion (see Table 4.1)

The remainder of the chapter takes a close look at the characteristics of major financial derivative products: forwards, futures, options, caps, collars, floors, and swaps.

FORWARDS

Forwards are agreements between two parties to exchange an underlying interest, suc'ı as a currency, a title, or a commodity at a specified future date and price. Forwards protect the two parties from price fluctuations of the underlying interest; the buyer against an increase in the price of the underlying interest; and the seller against a decrease in the price of underlying interest.

Forward contracts further specify the place and the conditions of delivery of the underlying object. Orange juice forward contracts, for instance, specify the factory warehouse or the supermarket, where the underlying orange juice quantity should be delivered. Foreign currency forwards specify a bank or a credit institution around the world, where the underlying currency should be deposited. Equity forward contracts specify a hypothecation institution where underlying shares should be delivered.

Table 4.1
Global Positions in OTC Derivative Markets by Type of Risk Instrument as of June 1998 (Billions of U.S. Dollars)

	Notional Amounts	Gross Market Values
Foreign Exchange Contracts	22,055	982
Interest Rate Contracts	24,124	1,354
Equity-linked Contracts	1,341	201
Commodity Contracts	506	39
Other	118	4

Source: Adopted from Bank of International Settlements (1999), p. 23.

For example, a U.S. computer hardware maker enters an agreement to purchase computer chips at a future date quoted in Japanese yen. The computer hardware maker can use a forward contract to "lock-in" a fixed dollar/yen exchange rate, in essence fixing the dollar price of the computer chips to be purchased.

Forward contracts are individualized contracts; that is, they cater to the needs of the two parties involved, do not trade in the secondary market, and are exercised only at settlement. Forward contracts are, normally, short-term contracts, extending up two years and, therefore, are suitable for hedging short-term risks, such as risks arising from short-term interest rate or foreign currency fluctuations.[1]

FUTURES CONTRACTS

Developed in the mid-1970s, futures contracts are standardized forward contracts; that is, agreements between two parties to exchange a standardized underlying interest, a foreign currency, an equity, a debt instrument at a future day and price. Thus, futures contracts can be classified as interest rate futures, foreign currency futures, equity futures, debt instrument futures, and so on.

In every future contract, the one party is the contract "writer" or seller, and the other party is the contract buyer. Futures contracts writers take a "short" position against the price of the underlying interest; that is, they expect the underlying interest to fall in price, while futures buyers take a "long" position; that is, they expect the price of the underlying interest price to fall. In this sense, futures contracts are bets on the direction of the price of the underlying interest within a certain time frame.

As standardized products, futures contracts cater to the general needs of a mass market rather than to the individual needs of a niche market, and trade in organized markets, which function as clearinghouses. The broadly applied U.S.–treasury bond futures trade in the Chicago Board of Trade (CBOT). Three-month Eurodollar futures trade in the Chicago Mercantile Exchange, and three-month Euromark futures trade in the London International Financial Exchange (LIFE).

In all traditional futures exchanges, trading follows an open outcry auction, that is, orders are openly announced and executed by exchange members. Open outcry provides for a fair, transparent, and efficient market, and guarantees that the two sides meet their obligations to each other. Futures exchanges collaborate with the futures clearinghouse, normally a separate corporation that facilitates the transaction of futures contracts; that is, the netting of short and long positions on each particular contract.[2]

To ensure that futures market participants fulfil their obligations to each other, futures exchanges further require members to comply with government futures rules and regulations, such as initial and subsequent "margin" requirements: The maintenance is by each of the parties of clearinghouse stock, cash, or government securities deposits.

Initial margin requirements vary from contract to contract, ranging between 3 and 20 percent of the contract value. For financial futures, for instance, the margin ranges between 3 and 10 percent of the contract value, while for commodity futures it can reach 50 percent. The initial margin requirements, for instance, for an IOM S&P contract is $23,438, the requirement for a Chicago Board of Trade treasury bond contract is $2,700, and the requirement for a New York Merchantile Exchange crude oil contract is $1,620 (see Table 4.2).

As the value of futures contracts vary daily with market conditions, margin requirements are monitored and adjusted daily by the Futures Exchange where the corresponding contracts are trading. Known as *marking to the market*, such procedure adjusts margins deposits to reflect the gains or losses from the changes in market conditions of that day. If the future prices rise, for instance, the accounts of holders of long positions (contract buyers) will be credited by the amount of the gain while the accounts of the holders of short positions (contract sellers) will be charged by the amount of the loss. Conversely, if the futures price decline, holders of long futures positions will be debited by the amount of the loss, and holders of short positions will be credited by the amount of gain.

In addition to monitoring margin requirements, the rules of the Futures Exchange specify the future contract's parameters, size, time, and conditions of delivery, and minimal price ticks. The Chicago Board of Trade, for instance, sets the parameters for U.S. T-bonds futures contracts. The New York Mercantile Exchange sets the parameters for the commodity futures contracts (see Table 4.2).

Futures Hedging versus Speculation

Hedging

Futures hedging is the use of futures products to offset fluctuations in the cash value of the underlying interest. To hedge fluctuations in a foreign currency denominated position, for instance, a bank can short foreign currency futures, as in the following example.

Table 4.2
Selective Future Contract Margins as of May 13, 1999

Contract (Exchange)	Contract Size	Original Margins	Minimal Price Fluctuation (Tick)
S&P (IOM)	$500xIndex	$23,438	0.05 Index pts or $25
Treasury Bonds (CBOT)	$100,000	2,700	1/32 or $31.25
Crude Oil (NYME)	1,000 barrels	1,620	1 cent or $10.00
Natural Gas (NYME)	10,000 mln Mm Btu	2,565	1/10 cent or $10.00
Corn (CBOT)	5,000 bushels	540	¼ cent or $12.5
Soybeans (CBOT)	12,500,000	1,080	0.000001 or $12.50

In July, bank A plans to buy $20 million worth of British securities as soon as its current U.S. portfolio matures, three months later in September. The current exchange rate is $1.50 per British pound, while the September British pound futures trade at $1.48. The size of the contract is 62,500 British pounds.

To hedge its position against the prospect of British pound appreciation over the next three months, bank A can buy 320 ($20 mil/62,500 British pounds) futures at $1.48.

If the British pound appreciates against the dollar, the bank will pay more per pound in the cash market, but it will pay less per pound in the futures market; that is, losses in the cash market will be offset by gains in the futures market.

The efficiency of hedging depends on the correlation between the cash and the futures market. The higher the correlation between the two markets, the more effective the hedging of the underlying interest position is. However, hedging cannot be perfect, because changes in the cash market are not always reflected in changes in the futures markets.

Speculation

Speculation is the taking of positions on financial futures on their own, without holding offsetting positions on the underlying instrument (cash market); that is, the simple purchase or sale of financial derivatives.

Speculative positions in futures are like lottery tickets on a contingent event. Holders of these positions stand to reap huge rewards if the price of the underlying interest moves in the right direction at the right time, or suffer a great deal of loss if the price of the underlying interest moves in the wrong direction or moves in the right direction at the wrong time.

In short, futures contracts are standardized derivative products that allow their holders to bet on the direction of the price of the underlying interest. They can be used both as hedging and as speculative devices. They are subject to margin requirements that are often a drag against each party's capital, which is not the case with options.

OPTIONS

Options are contracts that provide their holders the right but not the obligation to buy or sell a number of units of an underlying interest, an individual equity or index, a commodity, a foreign currency, or a treasury security at a specified price for a specified period of time. A call option provides its owner the right but not the obligation to buy the underlying interest, while a put option provides its owner the right but not the obligation to sell the underlying interest (see Figure 4.1). The prespecified price at which the underlying interest is purchased or sold is called strike price; the prespecified time that the right is no longer in effect is called expiration date; while the market price, that is, what buyers pay for an option contract is called premium. Thus, every option contract is described by eight parameters: size, type, underlying interest, expiration date, strike price, exercise, settlement, and premium.

Contract Size

Contract size is the number of units of the underlying interest to be exchanged. As the underlying interest can vary, so is the size of the options contract. One American-style equity options contract, for instance, includes for 100 shares of the company the options contract is written. A NYNEX crude oil options contract includes 1,000 barrels of crude oil. An IMM Japanese yen options contract includes 12,500,000 yen.

Figure 4.1
Classification of Options Contracts

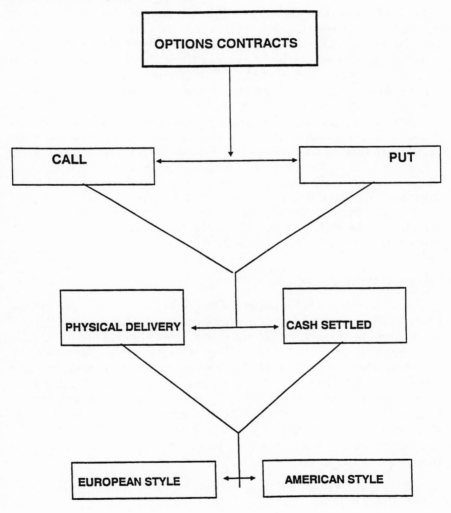

Contract Type

Options contracts are of two types, calls and puts, as defined earlier. Each contract type has a writer or seller and a buyer or holder.

Options Holders or Buyers

Option holders are the buyers of the rights specified in an option's contract. The holder of a physical delivery call option has the right but not the obligation to buy and receive physical delivery of the underlying interest within a certain period and at a prespecified price. The holder of one May NYNEX crude oil contract, for instance, has the right but not the obligation to receive physical delivery of 1,000 barrels of crude oil. Likewise, the holder of cash settled call has the right but not the obligation to receive a certain amount of cash (cash settlement) at exercise, without receiving the actual delivery of the underlying interest. The holder of an S&P 500 call contract, for instance, has the right but not the obligation to receive a certain amount of cash, which is determined by the difference between the strike price of the contract and the current price of the index. Likewise the holder of a physical delivery put option has the right but not the obligation to sell and deliver the underlying interest at a prespecified price.

Options Writers or Sellers

Options writers are the sellers of the rights specified in an option's contract. The writer of one physical delivery settled May NYNEX crude oil put contract, for instance, has the obligation to physically deliver 1,000 barrels of crude oil by the contract expiration date. Likewise, the writer of a cash delivery settled contract has the right but not the obligation to pay a certain amount of cash (cash settlement) at exercise, without actually delivering the underlying interest. The writer of an S&P 500 call contract, for instance, has the obligation to pay a certain amount of cash, which is determined by the difference between the strike price of the contract and the current price of the index.

Underlying Interest

Underlying interest is the commodity or the security title that is the subject of the options contract. Depending on the type of underlying interest, options can be classified in several categories, commodity, equities, currency, interest rate, debt, and so on.

- Stock or Equity Options are options on common stocks listed in major exchanges.
- Index Equity Options are options on major equity market indices, such as the S&P 100, the S&P 500, the FTSE, the Nikkei, and so forth.
- Debt Options are options on government or corporate debt. Debt options can be written on debt instrument prices (price-based) or on debt instrument yields (yield-based).
- Foreign Currency Options are options written on major foreign currencies, the Japanese yen, the German mark, the British pound, and so on.
- Commodity Options are options written on major commodity contracts, crude oil, wheat, soybeans, orange juice, metals, and so on.
- Future Contract Options are options written on futures contracts, currency futures contracts, commodity futures, and equity index futures.

Expiration Date

Expiration date is the date option contracts expire. If the option is not exercised on or before the expiration date, it is worthless. In the United States, for instance, expiration days for equity options and equity index options are set on the third Friday of each month in the three staggering cycles:[3]

1. The January/April/July/October cycle
2. The February/May/August/November cycle
3. The March/June/September/December cycle

Strike Price or Exercise Price

The exercise or strike price is the prespecified price at which the options holder and the options writer agree to exchange the underlying interest, commodity, equity, foreign currency, and so on. The owner of two XYZ 50 calls, for instance, has the right but not the obligation to buy 200 shares of corporation XYZ at $50. Conversely, the owner of two XYZ 50 put contracts has the right but not the obligation to sell 200 shares of the said corporation at $50.

To limit the number of available contracts, strike prices are normally set at five-point intervals for stocks selling below $60, ten-point intervals for stocks selling between $60 and $200, and twenty-point intervals for stocks above $200.

Exercise and Settlement

Depending on the way they are exercised, options are classified into two categories, physical delivery options, and cash settled options (see

Figure 4.1). Physical delivery options provide their holders the right to buy and receive delivery, in the case of calls, or sell and deliver, in the case of puts, the underlying interest. Cash settled options provide their holders the right to receive a certain amount of cash, the difference between the price of the underlying interest at the time the option is exercised and the strike price of the option contract.

Depending on the exercise time, options are classified in three categories, American-style options, European-style options, and capped options. American-style options can be exercised at any time from the time they are issued until the expiration date. European-style options can be exercised at the expiration time only. Capped options are exercised automatically before the expiration date, provided that certain conditions are satisfied.

Premium

Premium or option price is the sum that options holders must pay per contract to options writers, and is determined by demand for and the supply of that contract, which in turn depend on the price of the underlying interest vis-à-vis the contract strike price, the remaining time to expiration (option life), the expectations of investment buyers and sellers, and the volatility of the underlying interest.

The Price of the Underlying Interest vis-à-vis the Contract Strike Price

For call contracts, the further above the strike price the underlying interest trades, the higher the premium. For put contracts, the further below the strike price the underlying interest trades, the higher the premium. Thus, call contracts rise in price as the underlying interest rises. As the price of the S&P 100 index increased between November 13–20, 1998, for instance, from 549 to 568.62, the November 540 calls increased from 13 to 19-3/8, while puts dropped from 4-1/4 to 1/16 (see Table 4.3).

A call contract is in the money if the underlying interest trades above the strike price, and out of the money if the underlying interest trades below the strike price. Likewise, a put contract is in the money if the underlying interest trades below the strike price, and out of the money if the underlying interest trades above the strike price. When the S&P 100, for instance, was trading at 549, the November 540 call was in the money, while the November 540 put was out of the money (see Table 4.3).

The price of in-the-money options consists of two parts, the intrinsic value, and the time value. The intrinsic value of an in-the-money call is the margin by which the stock price exceeds the strike price, while the intrinsic value of an in-the-money put is the margin by which the stock price is below the strike price. An out-of-the-money option's intrinsic value is zero. When the S&P 100 was trading at 549, for instance, the intrinsic value of the November 540 call was at $9, while the November 540 put was zero (see Table 4.3).

The time value of an option's contract is the difference between the option premium and intrinsic value. The intrinsic value of an option can be best seen at expiration day, when the time value is zero, and, therefore, the option's premium reflects just the intrinsic value of the option. Likewise, the time value of an option's contract can be seen best when the price of the underlying interest is equal to the strike price. When the S&P 100 was at 540, the value of the November 540 call was at $4, while the value of the November 540 put was at 4-1/4 (see Table 4.3).

The Remaining Time to Expiration (Option Life)

For every option contract, the longer the remaining time to expiration, the higher the time value component of the premium. Conversely, the shorter the time, the smaller the time value component. On August 1, for instance, the value of a December call or put is higher than the value of a November or a September put.

The relationship is not linear, however; that is, the price of the option does not fall at a steady rate with time, it rather drops at a slower pace earlier on and at a faster pace later on (see Figure 4.2).

The Expectations of Investment Buyers and Sellers (Writers)

For put options buyers (writers), the larger the expected decline in the value of the underlying interest, the larger the put premium they are willing to pay (expect to receive). For call options buyers (sellers), the larger the expected increase in the price of the underlying interest, the higher the premium they are willing to pay (expect to receive).

The Volatility of the Underlying Interest

A high volatility in the price of the underlying interest is normally associated with high returns and high losses. Thus, the more

Table 4.3
S&P Market Value and Option Premiums
(November 13–November 20, 1998)

Index	Month	Strike Price	Call	Put
As of the close of Nov 13				
549	Nov.	540	13	4 1/4
549	Nov.	545	10 5/8	5 1/2
549	Nov.	550	7 ½	7 1/2
As of the close of Nov 16				
554.26	Nov.	540	17 ½	2 7/16
554.26	Nov.	545	14	3 3/8
554.26	Nov.	550	9 ¾	4 3/4
As of the close of Nov 18				
560.93	Nov.	540	22 5/8	13/16
560.93	Nov.	545	17	1 1/8
560.93	Nov.	550	12 ¾	1 5/8

volatile the price of the underlying interest, the higher the premium buyers (sellers) are willing to pay (receive).

In short, options contracts are complex financial products defined by a number of parameters: size, type, underlying interest, expiration date, strike price, exercise and settlement, and price.

Table 4.3 (*continued*)

Index	Month	Strike Price	Call	Put

As of the close of Nov 19

Index	Month	Strike Price	Call	Put
564.63	Nov.	540	23 ¼	5/16
564.63	Nov.	545	18 3/8	5/16
564.63	Nov.	550	16 5/8	½

As of the close of Nov 20

Index	Month	Strike Price	Call	Put
568.62	Nov.	540	29	1/16
568.62	Nov.	545	25 ¼	1/8
568.62	Nov.	550	19 3/8	3/16

Source: Adopted from the *Wall Street Journal*, November 14, 17, 19, 20, and 21, 1998.

Options Markets

As is the case with futures contracts, options contracts are traded in organized financial derivatives markets, such as the Chicago Board of Options Exchange and the Philadelphia Options Exchange in the United States and the European Options Exchange in Amsterdam. Each exchange has a clearinghouse or Options Clearing Corporation that executes orders on behalf of the exchange members (brokers dealers).

As is the case with common exchanges, to ensure the fair and orderly execution of options orders and minimize credit risks, options exchanges are subject to a number of self- or government-imposed rules and regulations. Brokers dealers, for instance, are not allowed to take positions on an options contract ahead of their clients (front running). Options holders are subject to limits as to the number of shares of a specific contract they can hold at a time.

Figure 4.2
Time Value of an Option's Contract

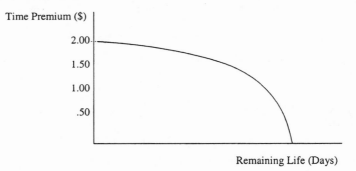

Options Orders

Due to the multiple contract option characteristics, option orders are complex, and often tricky for the inexperienced market participant.

Options orders are of two types: "open a position," which establishes a new position; and "close a position," which off-sets an established position. "Open a position" orders can be buy orders, establishing a long position or sell orders, establishing a short position. Likewise, "close a position" orders can be either buy orders, off-setting an open short position, or sell orders off-setting a long open position:

Open		Close
Buy	Establishing a long position	Offsetting a short position
Sell	Establishing a short position	Establishing a long position

For example, an order may be placed:

- "Buy three XYZ November 50 puts to open." The order establishes a long position, which consists of three contracts (300 shares) of company XYZ.
- "Sell three XYZ November 50 puts to close." The order closes the long position opened earlier.
- "Sell three XYZ November 50 puts to open." The order establishes a short position on the stock of company XYZ.

- "Buy three XYZ November 50 puts to close." The order closes the short position opened earlier.

Options: Risks versus Rewards

Option contracts are timely bets on the direction of the price of the underlying interest. And as is the case with conventional lottery bets, options holders stand to reap a big reward if the underlying interest moves in the right direction within the right time, or lose all or part of the money placed on the bet (option premium) if the price of the underlying interest either moves in the wrong direction or in the right direction at the wrong time. For example, an investor buys three company XYZ July 50 calls at $6. What are the maximum gains or losses from this contract?

The maximum loss is the premium $1,800 (3 × 100 × 6) plus commission, when the price of company XYZ stock falls sufficiently for the options contract to expire as worthless. Since the upside potential of the stock price of company XYZ is unlimited, the maximum gain is unlimited.

Another example is the case of an investor who buys three company XYZ July 50 puts at $6. What are the maximum gains and losses from this contract?

Again, the maximum loss is the premium paid to buy the contract; that is, $1,800 (3 × 100 × 6) plus commission. This loss is realized if the price of company XYZ stock rises sufficiently above the strike price for the option's contract to expire as worthless. Since the lowest price of a company stock is zero, the maximum gain for the option's buyer is the difference between the strike price and zero, that is 3 × 100 × 50 = $15,000.

Options: Hedging versus Speculation

As bets on the direction of the underlying interest, options can be used both as speculative and as hedging devices. As speculative devices options can buy or sell options contracts without taking an off-setting position in the underlying interest. In that case, options can result in substantial gains or losses. As hedging devices, options contracts can be purchased or sold in conjunction with off-setting positions in the underlying interest. Investors, for instance, who hold 300 shares in company XYZ can sell three put contracts, hedging their position against the prospect of a decline in the price of the stock of company XYZ. Conversely, investors who are 300 shares short in the stock of company XYZ can purchase three call contracts hedging their position against the prospect of a rise in the price of the stock of company XYZ.

The maximum gains and losses on options contracts are as listed in the following chart:

	Calls	Puts
Buyers—Maximum gains	Unlimited	The value of underlying interest
Buyers—Maximum losses	Premium	Premium
Sellers—Maximum gains	Premium	Premium
Sellers—Maximum losses	Unlimited	The value of underlying interest

Option Strategies

Option strategies are combinations of contracts to take advantage of expected market moves, such as covered calls and puts, naked calls and puts, straddles, strangles, and strips.

A covered call is the simultaneous purchase of an underlying title and the writing (selling) of call contracts on it, for example, the purchase of 200 shares of the stock of corporation XYZ and the sale of two calls on XYZ. Thus, covered calls offer investors both an opportunity for enhancing their portfolio income, and a limited downside protection. At the same time, they can limit the gain potential if the underlying stock appreciates substantially. For example, on January 2, an investor buys 200 shares of company XYZ, and sells two May 50 calls at $5 to open a position. What is the investor's net cost? What will happen to the investor's portfolio should the price of the stock of company XYZ falls to $40 at the time the option expires and the investor sells the stock? What if the price of the stock trades at $60 when the option expires or the investor closes its position?

Assuming commissions away for simplicity, the strategy's cost is as follows:

Stock Acquisition:	200 ($50) = $10,000
Receipts from the Option Sale:	2 (100) ($5) = $1,000
Net Cost	$9,000

Scenario 1:
The Stock Price Falls to $40

Receipts from the sale of the stock	200 ($40) = $8,000

Note that since the stock stays below the strike price at expiration, the option expires worthless; that is, the seller keeps the entire premium. Thus, the investor loses the total of $1,000, instead of $2,000 as would have been the case had he not written the two option contracts.

Scenario 2:
The Stock Price Is at $60 When the Investor Closes Its Position

Receipts from the stock sale:	200 × $60 = $12,000
Minus Cost	$9,000
Profit	$3,000

A naked call is the writing (sale) of call contracts without owning the underlying titles, which is a high risk/high reward strategy. The investor's gains are limited to the amount of the premium, while the losses are unlimited.

Straddle

A straddle is a transaction in which an investor buys both a call and a put with the same expiration date and strike price.

A good example of a straddle is the purchase of an XYZ August 40 call and an August 40 put, when the underlying interest trades at the strike price, which is at 40.

Spread

A spread is a transaction in which an investor buys one option and sells another option with different expiration dates on the same underlying interest.

Spreads positions can be "bull," "bearish," or "butterflies," and taken either on call contracts or on put contracts.

Bull Call Spread

A bull call spread is the simultaneous purchase of a call and the sale of another call with higher strike price and the same expiration date. Bull call spreads allow investors to gain from increases in the price of the underlying interest assuming a low risk. A good example of a bull spread is the purchase of an XYZ July 40 call and the sale of an XYZ July 45 call, when the underlying interest trades at 40.

Bear Call Spread

A bear call spread is the simultaneous purchase of a call and the sale of another call with lower strike price and the same expiration date. Bear call spreads allow investors to gain from declines in the price of the underlying interest at a low risk. A good example of a bear call spread is the purchase of an XYZ July 45 call and the sale of an XYZ July 40 call, when the underlying interest trades at 43.

Butterfly Call Spread

A butterfly call spread is the combination of a bull and a bear call spread. Thus, a butterfly position is a neutral position regarding the price movements of the underlying interest. It is therefore suitable for investors expecting the price of the underlying interest to remain within a narrow range.

Bull Put Spread

A bull put spread is the simultaneous purchase of a put of lower strike price (below the current market price), and the sale of another put of a higher strike price and the same expiration dates. A good example of a bear put spread is the buying of a company XYZ November 40 put and the sale of a company XYZ November 50 put, when the underlying stock price trades at $45.

Bear Put Spread

A bear put spread is the simultaneous sale of a put of a lower strike price, and the purchase of another put of a higher strike price and the same expiration dates. A good example of a bear put spread is the buying of a company XYZ November 50 put and the sale of a company XYZ November 40 put, when the underlying stock price trades at $45.

The butterfly put spread is a combination of a bull and a bear put spread.

The advantages and disadvantages of selective options strategies are as follows:

Strategy	Advantage	Disadvantage
Straddle	Big gain	Moderate risk
Covered call	Moderate gain	Moderate risk
Naked call	High gain potential	High risk

Bull call spread	Bet on a major upward move	High premium
Bear call spread	Bet on a major downward move	High premium
Butterfly call spread	Low premium	Limited protection

In short, options are rights, but not obligations to buy or sell an underlying interest at a predetermined price and time period. When used in conjuction with counter-positions in the underlying interest, options offer an efficient and effective way of hedging fluctuations in the price of the underlying interest. Yet options are short-term hedging investments, which is not the case with swaps.

SWAPS

Developed with the acceleration of the financial market liberalization in the 1980s, swaps are exchanges of payment flows involving two parties having an asymmetric multiperiod market exposure, one party is exposed to rising prices, and the other party is exposed to lower prices. The market exposure can be on the asset side, the liability side, or both sides of each party's balance sheet, and the swap allows the two parties to hedge their positions against a certain risk.[4]

Depending on the underlying interest, swaps can be classified in various categories, interest rate swaps, foreign currency swaps, total swaps, and so on. Irrespective of their use, swaps must meet the following conditions: the existence of an underlying instrument that creates asymmetric flows and the existence of two parties with asymmetric expectations regarding the direction of the price of the underlying instrument. Interest swaps, for instance, must satisfy three conditions:

1. The existence of both a loan (debt obligation) and an investment (claim) that create interest flows.
2. The existence of two parties, the one willing to borrow or invest in a product with a fixed interest income stream, and the other party willing to borrow or invest in a product with a variable interest income stream.
3. Interest rates must be favorable to the two parties.

CAPS

Caps are derivative products that impose an upper limit on price fluctuations of underlying interest or capital flows. Interest rate caps, for instance, impose a limit on the highest interest rate on a floating income or payment stream, such as a variable mortgage. Thus, caps work as European-style options based instruments. A typical interest rate cap starts at the spot or forward market, extends for a period of ten years, is structured in a bullet or amortizing form, applies any floating rate index, sets strikes at constant or variable levels, and can be reset at any time interval. Thus, interest rate caps protect their buyers against sharp interest rate increases at any period they remain in effect.

FLOORS

Floors are derivative products that set a lower limit on price fluctuations of underlying interest. Interest rate floors, for instance, set the lowest interest rate on a floating income or payment stream, such as a variable deposit. Thus, as was the case with caps, floors work as European-style options. A typical interest rate floor extends for a period of ten years, is structured in a bullet or amortizing form, applies any floating rate index, sets strikes at constant or variable levels, and can be adjusted at any time. Thus, while in effect, interest rate floors offer their buyers protection against sharp interest rate decreases.

COLLARS

Collars are derivatives that combine a cap and a collar, setting a price fluctuation range to protect their buyers against sharp interest rate increases or decreases at any period they remain in affect. An interest rate collar, for instance, sets an interest rate range on a floating payment or income stream. Thus, as was the case with caps and floors, collars work as European-style options. A typical interest rate floor extends for a period of ten years, it is structured in a bullet or amortizing form, applies any floating rate index, sets strikes at constant or variable levels, and can be reset at any time interval.

SWAPTIONS

Swaptions are combinations of swaps and options. They provide their holders the right but not the obligation to enter a swap transaction within a prespecified price and time period. A typical swaption is a fixed rate payer or receiver, it can be exercised in an American or European style, it can be written on any swap contract, it can strike at constant or adjustable levels, it can extend up to three years, and can be settled in a cash or swap form.

At this point, it should be emphasized, however, that financial derivatives should not be used as substitutes, but as complements for conventional risk management methods. As Haight and Kelly (1995) put it: "It should be emphasized that derivatives are not to replace traditional approaches to asset/liability management but should be used in conjunction with them" (p. 25). It should be further emphasized that financial derivatives allow banks and financial investors to shift risks, but they have not necessarily made the banking and the investment community a safer, risk-free world, especially when derivatives are used as bets against the efficiency of financial markets, that is, for speculation. "Derivatives are the fastest-growing financial instruments of our time. When used strategically, they can be very effective tools to mitigate risks. When used for speculation, that is, to bet on the efficiency of financial markets, they can be trouble, especially if you are unaware that you are betting" (Minehan and Simons 1995, 3–25). In 1992, the manager of Quantum Fund, George Soros, made over a billion dollars by betting successfully on a depreciation of the British pound. Conversely, unsuccessful derivative betting can spell disaster. In 1995, Nicholas Leeson, for instance, a Singapore-based trader for the Barings Bank of London, lost $1.3 billion of the bank's funds betting on the direction of the Nikkei equity index, eventually bringing an over-a-century-old bank down. A New York–based trader for Daiwa Bank lost $1.2 billion in commodity futures with the bank barely surviving such a loss. In 1996, Zahid Ashraf lost about $150 million of family funds in foreign currency trading. Procter and Gamble, Orange County in California, and Long-Term Capital have all lost a great deal of money in financial derivatives.

Financial derivative losses have alerted both bank management and regulators who by now have introduced legislation that requires the disclosure of financial derivative positions as "off-balance sheet" items. In 1992, for instance, the Swiss-based Bank of International Settlements (BIS) published what is known as the Basle Committee Report highlighting the growth of financial derivatives and laid down a number of rules to measure and manage financial risks, especially market risks. One such measure is the risk-adjusted capital adequacy capital requirements: riskier assets command higher capital requirements. In 1993, the Bank of England published its own report outlining some general regulation standards for the derivative markets. In 1994, the U.S. General Accounting Office published its own guidelines about the functioning of financial derivatives, requiring that banks prepare "a condition of income" report that discloses all "off-balance sheet" positions, such as financial derivatives. In 1993, the EU Directive 93/6 dealt with the capital adequacy of banks, including a provision for the risk of derivatives, and imposed a minimum capital adequacy ratio of 8 percent for all European Union banks and securities firms. In 1998, the Financial Accounting Standard Board issued Financial Accounting Standards No. 133 that sets the accounting and reporting guidelines for financial derivatives.[5]

Regulators have further cooperated informally with the banking and securities industries to rescue hedging funds. In 1998, "to enhance the probability of an orderly private-sector adjustment," the Federal Reserve Bank of New York mediated an agreement among banks and securities houses to bail out Long-term Capital Fund, avoiding the repercussions from an outright collapse.

In short, modern off-balance sheet risk management has a broad array of financial derivative products at its disposal. Each financial derivative has its own advantages and disadvantages. Forward contracts normally cater to specialized short-term risk management needs that are not covered by organized markets; and are premium free. Futures contracts normally cater to short-term general risk management needs, trade in organized exchanges, and are premium free. Options also cater to general short-term risk management needs, trade in organized exchanges, and bear a premium. Swaps normally cater to specialized long-term risk management needs, do not trade in organized exchanges, and do not bear a premium. Caps, floors, collars, and swaptions normally cater to specialized medium-term risk management needs; they do not trade in organized exchanges; and they bear a premium.

The advantages and the disadvantages of each instrument also determine applications as hedging devices. Banks concerned about the prospect of higher interest rates can enter FRA agreements, sell Eurodollar futures, buy interest-rate calls, caps, and sell floors. Banks concerned with foreign currency appreciation can buy foreign currency futures and options, an issue to be further addressed in subsequent chapters.

NOTES

1. As customized products, forward contracts can be extended for any number of years. Yet they are often used to protect their holders for adverse factors anticipated in the near future, from three to twenty-four months.

2. The clearinghouse in essence assumes the counterparty risk.

3. Option contracts actually expire on the third Saturday of the expiration month. Thus, the third Friday is the last day before these options contracts can trade before their expiration.

4. As OTC products, swaps allow their holders to shift a certain risk to the other party. Thus, they eliminate one risk, but create another, the counterparty risk; that is, the risk of one party failing to fulfill its contractual obligations to the other party.

5. Derivative instruments, for instance, should be reported in financial statements at their fair market values.

5

Credit Risk Management

> Derivatives cannot reduce the risks that go with owning volatile assets, but they can determine who takes on the speculation and who avoids it.
>
> Peter L. Bernstein (1998)

In 1989, economists at Olympic Bank, a major Greek commercial loan bank, grew concerned about its rapidly growing loan portfolio in the emerging economies of the Balkan region and the credit risk exposure associated with it. In particular, bank economists raised doubts about the ability of a number of corporate borrowers in the region to repay their loans due to deteriorating domestic macroeconomic conditions.

Olympic Bank's problem is neither new nor unique. As the extension of credit has always been at the core of the banking operations, credit risk management has been the focus of banking risk management, and that applies both to the bank loan and to the investment portfolio. Banks must carefully craft their lending strategy, screen their borrowers, determine the investment and lending terms and conditions, and monitor closely their will and ability to repay their debt.

Addressing credit-risk management in more detail, this chapter reviews conventional and modern credit-risk management methods, in two sections. The first section is a discussion of "credit scoring and ranking," a broadly applied "on-balance sheet" credit risk management method. The second section is a discussion of "off-balance sheet" methods and credit derivatives, especially credit swaps and options.

CREDIT SCORING AND RANKING

Credit scoring and ranking is a conventional credit risk management method that reviews and analyzes borrowers' financial status, and classifies them to risk ranks that determine the loan terms and conditions. In this sense, "risk ratings are the primary summary indicator of risk for banks' individual credit exposures. They both shape and reflect the nature of credit decisions that banks make daily" (Treacy and Carey 1998, 897).

Credit-risk rating can be performed both externally, by credit reporting agencies, and internally, by banks' own staff. Credit-risk rating for government and corporate debt is usually performed by major credit reporting agencies, such as Moody's, and S&P. Moody's, for instance, classifies debt instruments in several categories, from Aaa, debt of best quality (U.S. government debt, blue-chip corporate debt), to C, debt of extremely poor quality. S&P classifies debt from AAA, debt with almost certain principal and interest payments, to D, debt with either principal or interest payments in arrears.

Credit-risk rating for individual and corporate loans is usually performed internally by experienced credit officers who monitor closely the economic and financial performance of the existing and prospective clients.

Developed internally, individual and corporate credit scoring and ranking systems are often proprietary systems, rarely revealed to outsiders, so it is difficult to come up with a general description of the method. Bearing this limitation in mind, this section provides a "typical" credit scoring and ranking system, underscoring the ex post levers that banks apply to minimize the subjective nature of the method.

As can be recalled from the previous chapters, credit risk is about the probability that borrowers fail to make timely interest or principal payments to their creditors. Credit risk stems from the borrowers' failure to comply with a loan agreement, the breaching of financial covenant or other loan condition and is present in any kind of financial exposure; that is, in loans, debt, and equity investment. Thus, credit risk depends on a number of microindustry or borrower-specific economic and financial conditions and on a number of large-scale economic conditions, which determine the borrowers' credit worthiness; that is, the ability and determination to repay their debts.

Microconditions include a number of industry characteristics, such as the product and resource supply and demand conditions that determine the company's narrow business environment, and a number of economic and financial company-specific characteristics, such as profit margins, market share, financial leverage, and cash flows, as briefly discussed in Chapter 3. Macroconditions include a number of economywide characteristics, such as the state of the economy, demographic trends, and so on that determine the company's broader business environment.

Credit-risk management consists of a collection and analysis of micro- and macro-data to evaluate credit requests and to determine borrowers' credit worthiness, and the terms and conditions for hedging the bank's loan and investment positions. Specifically, in the case of loans, credit-risk management begins with credit requests by existing or new customers that come under the scrutiny of separate lending departments, which collect and analyze information about customers' credit worthiness.

The analysis of credit requests is a very important phase of commercial bank lending. In large banks a separate department is sometimes maintained, under the supervision of the loan department, to collect information regarding borrowers, to prepare and analyze information in order to determine the credit worthiness or business under investigation, and to keep credit information for future use. (Reed 1963, 50)

Credit-risk management continues with the second stage, where the bank sets forth its credit objectives, especially the trade-off between risk and reward, which results in the definition and specification of credit risk ranks, say, A, B, C, D, E, F. Each class represents a certain degree of credit risk, a probability of losses (principal and interest); and determines the terms and conditions of the loan, including interest rate premium, hedging, and monitoring requirements. Class A, for instance, is saved for low risk clients, normally blue chip companies with solid economic and financial fundamentals that score high on the evaluation criteria mentioned earlier. Credit class B is saved for customers of low to moderate risk. Credit class C is saved for medium to average risk, and so on.

Once the credit-risk ranks are defined and specified, credit-risk management proceeds with the third stage, the organization of customer's quantitative and qualitative data in group categories, sales and profit growth, loan type and amount request; financial structure, net worth, liquidity, cash flow; and profit margins; and efficiency, as briefly discussed in Chapter 3. Each group category is assigned a grade from a grade scale, and grades from all categories are summed up to derive a total score, which in turn is divided with the number of group categories to determine the average customer score:

$$\text{Average Total Score} = \frac{\text{Sum of Group Grades}}{\text{Number of Group Categories}}$$

Once the average total score is determined, the customer is classified in one of the predetermined classes, as discussed earlier. Customers with a high average score are classified in class A. Customers with a somewhat lower score are classified in class B, while customers with still lower scores are classified in lower classes.

It must be emphasized that the choice of the evaluation criteria, their grouping into separate categories, the choice of grade scales for each group are subjective, a matter of experience and judgment by the credit officer or the credit committee that is performing this exercise. Thus, "the rating process almost always involves the exercise of human judgment because the factors considered in assigning a rate and the weight given each factor can differ significantly across borrowers" (Treacy and Carey 1998, 898). Nevertheless, in the process of evaluation, some factors or criteria could be weighted, provided that the weights are explained and justified. The criteria should be evaluated for a minimum period of three years and the grade should be based on the trend in each group for that period and compared to certain industry standards.

To illustrate the scoring and ranking method, the following are group evaluation criteria. The grading scale for each group category is set from 0 to 4. Thus, the maximum total score that a customer can receive is 40, and the minimum is 0. And since the number of group categories is 10, the average total score is also between 0 and 4.

1. Sales and profit growth—loan type and amount requested
2. Financial structure—net worth, liquidity, cash flow
3. Profit margins—efficiency

4. Form of organization—management quality
5. Market position—competition
6. Years and quality of relationship with bank, debtors, creditors
7. Economic sector (industry)—geographical location
8. Machinery—equipment quality, investment programs
9. Planning, marketing, R&D
10. Quality and suffiency of collected information
    Total score
    Classification
    Default history—nonperforming loans
    New classification
    Collateral

Depending on the bank's policy objectives, the degree of loan portfolio risk it is willing to assume, a score range and a decision benchmark is set. In this example, customers who receive a score between 3.1 and 4.0 are classified in risk class A. Customers who receive a score between 2.1 and 3.0 are classified in class B, and customers who receive a score between 1.1 and 2.0 are classified in class C (see Table 5.1). Customers in all three classes are approved, while

Table 5.1
Scoring and Asset Classification

Risk Class	Grades	Assets at
A	3.1 to 4	Very Low Risk
B	2.1 to 3	Low to Moderate Risk
C	1.1 to 2	Medium to Average Risk
D	0 up to 1	High Risk
E	no grade	Very High Risk
F	no grade	Default

customers in D are rejected, and classification in E and F are reserved for the reclassification process.

After the bank derives customer scores and classifies them into respective categories, risk management advances to the fourth stage, the setting of the loan terms and conditions. Customers classified in class A, for instance, could be assigned a relatively low rate, for example, the prime rate, and subject to infrequent financial reviews and collateral evaluation, say, annually. Customers in credit class B could be assigned a higher interest rate (risk premium), for example, a few basis points over the prime, and subject to frequent financial and collateral reviews and evaluation, say, twice a year; and customers in class C could be assigned even higher interest rates, and subject to even more frequent review and evaluation, say, quarterly.

- *Credit Class A: Very Low Credit Risk.* Financial analysis and evaluation once a year; collateral evaluation once a year;[1] credit score estimation, either right after the financial analysis or at any time after a new loan demand.
- *Credit Class B: Low to Moderate Credit Risk.* Financial analysis and evaluation twice a year includes estimation; collateral evaluation twice a year; and credit score estimation right after the financial analysis or at any time after a new loan demand.
- *Credit Class C: Medium to Average Credit Risk.* Financial analysis and collateral evaluation once every three months; credit score estimation right after the financial analysis or at any time after a new loan demand.
- *Credit Class D: High Credit Risk.* Customer under continuous monitoring and reevaluation.
- *Credit Class E: Nonperforming or Bad Loans.* Customer in default of part or total interest and principal outstanding; loan is not normally served; bank takes legal actions to recover the loan.
- *Credit Class F (losses).* Customers in default and insolvency. The total amount of loan is considered a loss and the bank must write off the total amount.

Credit scoring and ranking does not apply to new customers only. It extends to existing customers, who are regularly evaluated and upgraded or downgraded, and reclassified in risk classes when requesting a new loan or the renewal of a revolving credit line. As with new customers, if reclassified in the first class, their loans are considered as "normal assets," and their credit application are approved (see Table 5.1). If classified in class B, their loans are considered as "performing with some risk," and their credit applications are approved. If classified in class D, their applications are not approved, and they are placed under close monitoring, and eventually classified under classes E or F.

For customers classified in the last two risk ranks, the bank imposes additional requirements before it takes further action, which depends on whether the credit request comes from a new or an existing client.

1. New customer: The credit request is not approved until collateral offered is inspected and evaluated.
2. Existing customer: The credit request is not approved until collateral offered is inspected and evaluated. The bank may treat existing loans in default and take legal action to secure repayment in full.

Irrespective of the type of customer, credit scoring and ranking is not a terminal, but an ongoing process that monitors each loan and each class of loans until they are repaid in full. Thus, banks amass enormous statistical information, which allows them to estimate the probability distribution of loan defaults and delinquencies for each risk class. Once such probability distribution is estimated, banks know with high degree of accuracy the credit risk it assumes in each risk class. This knowledge of credit risk, in turn, is followed by the review and revision of credit policy, and most notably the revision of credit scores. Banks, for instance, who find that they assume too high a credit risk in class A, can adjust their score range upward. If the bank in the earlier example, for instance, decides to lower its risk exposure, it can adjust its scoring by classifying in risk class A only customers receiving a grade from 3.5 up to 4.0 instead of 3.1 up to 4.0, and eventually deny credit to those who would be approved under the old system. Thus, some of the customers classified in class A under the old scoring range are now classified in class B. Alternatively, banks may decide to raise the risk premium for the risk class customers found to be at higher risk than initially thought, or ask for additional collateral;[2] and can impose covenants with certain requirements as to how the borrower can use profits or sales proceeds.[3]

In short, credit scoring and ranking is an internal procedure that screens bank borrowers according to a number of quantitative and qualitative characteristics such as sales, profit growth, market share growth, financial structure, organization, and the length and the quality of relations with the bank are classified in growth categories and graded to derive an average total score.

This score, in turn, is applied to place customers in prespecified risk classes, which determine whether the customer qualifies for the loan, as well as the terms and the conditions of the loan. Customers classified in low risk classes are approved and assigned favorable loan terms conditions, while customers assigned in middle- to high-income classes are either rejected or assigned less favorable loans terms and conditions. But what if a bank enters a new market where information about new customers is limited, and of poor quality, as is the case in many emerging markets? The bank can hedge its positions; that is, mitigate credit risks with credit derivatives, as will be discussed in the following section.

CREDIT DERIVATIVES

As discussed in the previous chapters, off-balance sheet risk management methods, such as financial derivatives, have been primarily developed for managing market risks and most notably currency and interest rate risks that businesses and banks have been facing in a global deregulated economy while credit risk continued to be managed with conventional on-balance sheet methods.

Since 1992, as banks and investors have in general expanded lending to the emerging economies where microeconomic and macroeconomic data are of poor quality and market conditions can change dramatically from one day to the next, a new class of financial derivatives has emerged to protect banks and investors in general against the prospect of borrower total or partial default, and credit default.

As is the case with other financial derivatives, credit derivatives derive value from an underlying interest, a credit instrument, a government or a corporate bond or a loan, and have an intrinsic value once certain contract conditions take effect. Thus, buyers of credit derivatives can hedge their positions against the prospect of a total or partial borrower default.

Depending on the hedging horizon, banks can apply a broad range of credit derivatives. For short-term hedging, for instance, banks can apply credit options, while for long-term hedging, they can apply credit swaps.

Short-Term Hedging: Credit Options

As defined in the previous chapters, options are derivative products that provide their holders the right but not the obligation to buy or sell an underlying interest at a specified price for a specified period of time. Credit options provide their holders the right but not the obligation to buy or sell an underlying debt instrument, pay or receive full payment for the principal of a loan, and therefore can be used as a hedge against credit risk. Some calls, for instance, allow their holders to receive payments that are inversely related to the credit rating of the borrower; that is, their value rises as the borrower's credit rating drops. Other calls, known as "digital default calls" allow their holders to collect the entire loan principle in the case of borrower default (Saunders 2000). Thus, credit options can serve as a form of credit insurance; that is, for a premium, allow lenders to shift credit risk to a third party.

By contrast to other options that are written on the price of an underlying interest, credit options are written on certain conditions that declare part or all debt payments in default, and, therefore, trigger the exercise of the option. Thus, credit option contracts must explicitly define the debt instrument, and the exercise and settlement conditions. Option contracts must further define the events that may trigger their exercise, which, as the September 1998 Russian debt crisis demonstrated, is a rather complex task.

Long-Term Hedging: Credit Swaps

As discussed in the previous chapters, in general, swaps are agreements between two parties to exchange two financial flows. A credit swap is an agreement to swap a debt payment for a fee, normally a percentage of the outstanding debt principle. Thus, credit swaps serve as a form of credit guarantee, substituting for other conventional risk management instruments, such as letters of credit. And as is the case with conventional swaps and letters of credit, banks must carefully screen their counterparties, especially for over-the-counter derivatives; that is, the ability and determination of the counterparty to fulfill its contractual obligations. In fact, banks entering credit risk swaps take an unusually high counterparty risk for two reasons. First, due to the lack of public information, the probability of default used in the swap pricing is more a guess rather than an objective estimate. Second, default values are often extremely high and difficut to be hedged by the counterparty (Park 1998, 30).

Concerned about the unusual counterparty risk, U.S. government regulators require that banks maintain capital against the risk of counterparty default (Seiberg 1997, 4). The capital to be maintained is estimated by multiplying the market value of the credit derivative with a factor that varies with the investment rating of the credit derivative: the higher the credit rating the lower the factor.

In general, the management of credit risk with credit swaps makes sense for a bank when

- a large portion of a bank's loans is earmarked to a specific sector; and, therefore, the bank is taking too high a risk.
- a large portion of loans is earmarked to a specific country; social and political events may have a negative impact on the economy of the country, and the ability of the borrowers of this country to repay their debt.
- the bank has a limited knowledge of a market, as is often the case when banks expand to emerging markets.
- the bank must reduce its credit risk in order to comply with government regulations.

The procedure of a pure credit swap is simple and includes two steps. In the first step, the first institution pays the second a fixed amount, normally a percentage of the notional principal. In return, the second institution assumes the obligation to pay off the remainder of the loan in case the borrower fails to do so.

To understand how credit swaps work, let us return to the situation of the Olympic Bank that is holding a large portfolio of corporate loans in the Balkan region. Olympic Bank can enter a swap with another bank in the region, an institution that has a better understanding of the economic and financial conditions of the region, say, the Balkan Bank, which is more familiar with the emerging markets of the Balkan region.

The credit swap between the two banks can take the following form: The first step is signing a credit swap agreement. Olympic Bank extends a loan to Corporation A. Then Olympic Bank and the Balkan Bank sign an agreement that, for a commission, Balkan Bank will repay the loan of Corporation A, in the case the said corporation fails to do so.

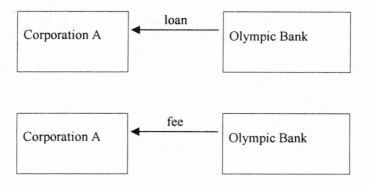

The second step is termination of the loan. The loan can be terminated in two ways. First, Corporation A repays it in full, the Balkan Bank keeps the swap fee. Second, corporation A fails to repay the loan, so the Balkan Bank pays it.

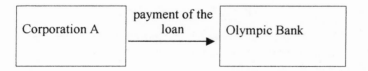

Or, in the case of failure of the company to repay the loan:

To sum up, for years, credit-risk management has traditionally been an on-balance sheet operation. Under a method known as credit scoring and ranking banks collected quantitative and qualitative information about the financial situation of their current and prospective clients, organized them in categories, assigned a grade to each category, and came up with average grade for all categories that classified each client into a risk class; and set the loan terms and conditions for each risk class. Clients in low risk classes were assigned low interest rate-risk premia, while clients in high risk classes were assigned high interest rate-risk premia or their loan or credit extension applications (existing clients) were rejected altogether.

In either case, banks monitored their loans closely, developed historical probabilities of loan defaults for each client category, and adjusted their scoring and ranking system accordingly. If scoring is adjusted upward, customers that had originally been classified in a low-risk class may now be classified in a high-risk class. Conversely, if scoring is adjusted downward, customers that had originally been classified in a high-risk class, may now be classified in a low-risk class.

In recent years, conventional risk management methods have been supplemented by modern off-balance sheet methods that use financial derivatives, such as credit options and swaps to transfer credit risk to third parties. This method is particularly useful to banks expanding in emerging economies where financial and economic information is limited and of poor quality, and therefore, conventional scoring and ranking cannot be reliable.

NOTES

1. Collateral could be any product that could be possessed and liquidated for the repayment of the loan, such as commercial or residential property, cash, debt or equity equities, collectables, letters of credit, and so on.

2. The size of interest rate is affected by the credit risk included in each financial product and is directly connected to the issuer of this product. The risk premium is reflected in the difference between the rate of a credit risk-free product, such as treasury bills, and the rate of risky products. The higher the risk the higher the risk premium. Banks usually set a range of interest rates starting from prime rate, for customers without credit risk or customers with low credit risk and go up to general rate for customers with high credit risk. Rates between prime rate and general rate are for customers with various degrees of credit risk.

3. Some loan covenants, for instance, require that the borrower distributes any profits before the loan is paid in full.

6

Interest Rate Risk Management

> Banks use derivative products mainly to manage interest rate risk; the increased volatility of interest rates has made the need for accurate measurement and control of interest rate risk particularly acute.
>
> Katerina Simons (1995, 24)

In the late 1980s, economists at the Olympic Bank, a major Greek bank, grew concerned about another problem, the rising government deficits and the prospect of higher short-term, medium-term, and long-term interest rates, which, if materialized, could have a negative impact on both the bank balance sheet and operations statement. In particular, bank economists were concerned about a large portion of the bank's fixed rate portfolio financed by floating rate funds borrowed in the interbank market.

Olympic Bank is not alone. In a deregulated economy, every bank and every financial institution is concerned with interest rate fluctuations. Higher interest rates, for instance, have a negative impact on banks as borrowers of funds at floating rates, such as money market accounts, short maturity CDs, banker's acceptances. In addition, higher interest rates have a negative effect on banks as lenders of funds at fixed interest rates and as investors in fixed income securities. Conversely, lower interest rates have a negative impact on banks as issuers of long-term CDs and holders of floating rate loans and investments. How can banks protect themselves from this unfavorable interest rate prospect?

As discussed in the previous chapters, to manage interest rate risk, banks must first measure their interest rate exposure; that is, determine the interest rate sensitivity of their assets and liability positions, and of their net income. Specifically, to determine the impact of interest rates on their asset and liability positions (position risk), banks must measure the duration and the convexity of their assets and liabilities. To determine the impact of interest rates on their net income (income risk), banks must measure the interest rate gap of their assets and liabilities. Banks with a fixed income asset portfolio of a relatively long duration, for instance, will assume a larger position risk, should interest rates rise, than banks with a comparable portfolio of a relatively short duration. Moreover, banks with a positive interest rate gap face a deterioration of their interest rate spread (net interest income) should interest rates fall (see Table 6.1). Conversely, banks with a negative interest rate gap face an improving interest rate spread should interest rates fall.

To protect their net worth and income against the prospect of interest rate fluctuations, banks can apply conventional on-balance sheet risk management methods; that is, restructure their assets and liabilities, so as to immunize or minimize the averse impact of rising interest rates, and even enhance the bank's net income.[1] To minimize the impact of interest rate fluctuations on their net worth, banks, for instance, expecting higher interest rates, can take measures to shorten the duration of their asset portfolio, and lengthen the duration of their liabilities. Conversely, banks which expect lower interest rates can take measures to lengthen the duration of their asset portfolio, and shorten the duration of their liabilities.

To minimize the impact of higher interest rates on their net income, banks can restructure both their assets and their liabilities. On the asset side, banks can substitute fixed rate assets, such as fixed rate mortgages and bonds for floating rate assets, such as adjustable rate mortgages, and business and consumer loans. On the liability side, banks can substitute floating rate for fixed rate liabilities (see Table 6.2). Likewise, to minimize the impact of lower interest rates on their net income banks can increase their fixed interest assets, reduce floating rate assets, or increase floating liabilities.

Supplementing conventional risk management measures, banks can apply a broad range of modern off-balance sheet measures, such

Table 6.1
Interest Rate Gaps, Interest Rate Fluctuations, and Revenue Changes

	Interest Rate Change	
Interest Rate Gap	Rise	Decline
Positive	Net Interest Revenue Rise	Net Interest Revenue Falls
Negative	Net Interest Revenue Falls	Net Interest Revenue Rise
Zero	Net Interest Revenue Unchanged	Net Interest Revenue Unchanged

as interest rate derivative instruments, treasury bond futures, caps, floors, swaps, and so on (see Table 6.3).[2] To minimize the impact of rising medium-term rates on the liability side, banks can enter cap agreements. To minimize the impact of rising long-term interest rates on its fixed rate loan portfolio, banks can enter a swap agreement. To minimize the impact of short-term interest rate rise on their liabilities, for instance, banks can enter FRAs and treasury futures, or buy treasury futures put options. Likewise, to minimize the impact of lower interest rate on their assets, banks can sell FRAs, buy treasury futures or treasury futures calls.

As of June 1998, interest rate swaps were the most broadly used interest rate derivatives, reaching a notional amount of $32,942 billion and a market value of $1,184 billion, followed by interest rate options, which reached a notional amount of $8,528 billion and a market value of $126 billion (see Table 6.4).

Each strategy has its own advantages and disadvantages, as discussed in Chapter 4. Conventional methods have a large transaction cost, and may result in large losses, especially if many banks

Table 6.2
Interest Rate Fluctuations and Selective On-Balance Sheet Risk
Management

Interest Rates are Expected to	Risk Management Strategy
Rise	Reduce fixed rate assets/
	Increase Floating rate assets
	Or reduce
	Floating rate liabilities/
	Increase fixed rate liabilities
Fall	Increase fixed rate assets/
	Reduce floating rate assets
	Or increase
	Floating rate liabilities/
	Decrease fixed rate liabilities

try to unwind the same positions at the same time. Modern techniques such as interest rate futures have a short life and require margin deposits, while interest rate options, caps, floors, and collars require a premium. Thus, the choice of policy mix depends on the bank objectives, such as the hedging horizon, transaction costs, and risk premium considerations.

Addressing the use of modern off-balance sheet risk management methods; that is, financial derivatives to manage interest rate risk, the remainder of the chapter is in three sections. The first section discusses the use of FRAs and IRFs to manage risks due to short-term interest rate fluctuations. The second section discusses the use of interest rate swaptions, caps, floors, and collars to manage risks due to medium-term interest rate fluctuations, and the third section discusses the use of interest rate swaps to manage risks due to long-term interest rate fluctuations.

Table 6.3
Interest Rate Fluctuations and Selective Off-Balance Sheet Risk Management

Interest Rates are Expected to	Risk Management Strategy
Rise	Buy FRAs
	Sell Treasury futures
	Buy Treasury futures puts
	Swap floating for fixed liabilities
	Buy caps on floating rate liabilities
Fall	Sell FRAs
	Buy Treasury futures
	Buy Treasury futures calls
	Swap floating for fixed assets
	Buy floors on floating rate assets

MANAGING SHORT-TERM INTEREST RATE RISKS: FORWARD RATE AGREEMENTS (FRAs), INTEREST RATE FUTURES (IRFs), AND OPTIONS

FRAs

Gaining in popularity in the early 1980s as an over-the-counter product, Forward Rate Agreements are agreements between two parties to enter a future loan transaction at a predetermined interest rate. The one party promises to lend the other party a notional principal at a predetermined interest rate, and therefore protects the one side from a rise and the other side from a decline in interest rates.

Table 6.4
Global Positions in OTC Interest Rate Derivatives as of June 1998 (Billions of U.S. Dollars)

	Notional Amounts	Gross Markets Values
FRAs	6,602	39
Swaps	32,942	1,184
Options	8,528	126
Other	52	2

Source: Bank of International Settlements, 1999, p. 23.

FRAs are simple, inexpensive, one-period interest rate risk-hedging instruments of a notional principal; that is, the payment flows exchanged are limited to interest payments only, not to the capital associated with these interest payments.

Every FRA contract has two parties, a buyer and a seller with asymmetric expectations on the future direction of interest rates; the one party expects interest rates to rise, while the other party expects interest rates to fall. The two parties enter an agreement to exchange interest payment flows at a predetermined interest rate that is different from the current prevailing market rate. The two parties further agree to an effective day, a settlement day, and a termination date:

Buyer: The FRA buyer is the party that seeks protection from a market interest rate increase. Thus, the buyer makes interest payments based on a notional principal and a fixed interest rate, the FRA rate. Thus, the FRA buyer borrows a certain principal at a predetermined fixed rate that must be repaid at a future date, and receives interest on the same notional principal based on a market interest rate, for example, the London International Borrowing Rate (LIBOR). At the same time, the buyer lends an equal principal at a variable rate. Thus, if the market interest rate is lower than the FRA, buyers lose money but have protected themselves from an interest rate increase (see Figure 6.1).

Seller: The FRA seller is the party that seeks protection from an interest rate decrease. Thus, the seller receives interest payments based on a

Figure 6.1
Buyer and Seller Losses in a Simple FRA

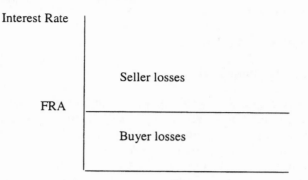

notional principal and a variable interest rate, for example, LIBOR or the FRA rate; the FRA seller lends a certain principal at market rates. At the same time, the buyer pays interest on the same notional principal based on a fixed interest rate, the FRA rate. Thus, if the market interest rate is lower than the FRA interest rate, sellers gain. Conversely, if interest rates end up higher, sellers lose but they protect themselves from interest rate decline (see Table 6.4).

FRA Interest Rate: The fixed rate agreed upon by the two sides.

Market Interest Rate or Future Interest Rate: The reference interest rate as it is determined by market conditions; that is, the LIBOR, Prime Rate, Commercial Paper Rate, and so on.

Effective Date of the FRA: The date the agreement goes into effect.

Settlement Date: The date of payment of interest rate difference.

Expiration Date of the FRA: The date the FRA expires.

Thus, the FRA life can be divided in two periods, one lasting from the signing of the contract to the settlement, and another from the settlement to the termination date. Normally, the length of the first period is one to twelve months, while the length of the second period is approximately three to twelve months.

In general, the settlement value is given by this formula:

$$\text{Settlement Amount} = (\text{FRA} - \text{FR}) * D * \text{NP}/360 * 100$$

where

FRA = FRA interest rate

FR = Future interest rate or reference interest rate

D = Number of days in period

NP = Notional principal

Bank A has made a six-month loan commitment to be assigned three months from now. The loan is for $10 million and the interest rate is the same as the prime rate, which is currently at 8 percent.

Concerned with the prospect of a rise in the prime rate for the next six months, Bank A can enter a six-month FRA (settled three months from today) with a counterpart, such as a bank or another company, at a fixed rate, say, 9 percent. Thus, the FRA allows Bank A to shift the risk of rising rates over the next three months to the counterparty, while it can benefit from a decline in interest rates. Specifically, if interest rates at a settlement date are above 9 percent, say, 10 percent, the counterparty will pay the difference, that is 1 percent or $50,000 (10,000,000 * [17% − 16%] / 2). Thus,

$$\text{Settlement Amount} = (9\% - 10\%) * 180 * \$10,000,000/(360 * 100)$$
$$= \$50,000$$

Since the payment is made in the beginning of the FRA period, the final payment must be discounted as follows:

$$\text{Discounted Settlement Amount} = \$50,000/[1 + (10\% - 9\%/2)]$$
$$= \$49,751.20$$

In short, FRAs are simple one-period interest rate hedging instruments. They allow banks to hedge interest rate risk for one period only, normally three months to a year, but have two major disadvantages. First, adjustments on the buyers' and sellers' positions are made at the settlement date, and therefore, the risk of one side failing to fulfill its contractual obligations is quite high. Second, FRAs do not trade in organized derivative markets, and therefore lack liquidity, which is not the case with IRFs.

IRFs

Introduced in 1976 with the writing of futures contracts on ninety-day and one-year U.S. Treasury bills, IRFs have emerged as standardized FRAs. They allow two parties to exchange a notional principal at a certain interest rate and trade daily in major futures exchanges. Treasury bond and treasury note futures, for instance, trade in the Chicago Board of Trade, while Eurodollar futures trade in the Chicago Mercantile Exchange.

To understand how futures hedging works, take a bank expecting a $10 million repayment three months from now, to be reinvested in thirty-year U.S. bonds, currently yielding 6.2 percent. The bank expects long-term interest rates to fall in the next three months, driving the thirty-year bond prices higher and yields lower. How can the bank protect itself against this prospect? By buying or taking a long position in three-month T-bond futures. Specifically, since bond futures are sold in $100,000 denominations, the bank can buy 100 T-bond futures contracts.

IRF contracts are issued at different sizes. Treasury bonds and note contracts are issued at $100,000 each, the Thirty-Day Federal Funds contracts at $5 million each, and the Eurodollar at $1 million each (see Table 6.5).

IRF contracts are settled on the expiration day, at a settlement price that is calculated by subtracting an annual interest rate from 100. IRF contracts also have a future price calculated by subtracting the settlement price from 100.

Trading on major exchanges, IRFs are subject to stringent government and exchange regulations to ensure market liquidity and transparency and prompt and accurate executions of transactions.

Table 6.5
Selective Interest Rate Futures

Product	Exchange	Introduced	Contract Size
US Treasury Bonds	CBOT	1977	$100,000
US Treasury Notes	CBOT	1982	$100,000
30-Day Federal Funds	CBOT	1986	$5 million
Eurodollar	CME	1981	$1 million
Eurodeutchemark	LIFFE	--	DM1 million

To provide for liquidity, for instance, exchanges have a clearing-house that executes and reports futures transactions. Exchanges further monitor and implement margin requirements and the mark-to-market, a procedure that adjusts those requirements to reflect changing market conditions.

A good illustration of how IRFs work and allow banks and investors in general to hedge their positions is the three-month Eurodollar IRF. Introduced in 1981 by the International Monetary Market (IMM), and a year later by the London International Financial Futures Exchange (LIFFE), Eurodollar IRF contracts are written on dollar-denominated deposits. The conventional IMM contract, for instance, is written on a $1 million three-month deposit. Interest rates are calculated on a 360-day year. Contracts are settled in cash upon delivery, and trades in the International Monetary Market (IMM), a division of the Chicago Merchantile Exhange.

IRFs expire in March, June, September, and December of every year. The settlement price is calculated by subtracting an average interest rate from 100:

$$\text{Settlement Price} = 100 - \text{Annual Interest Rate}$$

Conversely,

$$\text{Future Rate} = 100 - \text{Settlement Price}$$

Assuming, for instance, that the average interest rate on the settlement date is 7.25 percent, the settlement price is 92.75. Conversely, if the settlement price is 92.75, the future rate is 7.25 percent.

As is the case with other derivatives, IRF buyers take a long position, while sellers take a short position; that is, have the obligation to pay the underlying interest at a predetermined strike price. IRFs are also subject to the standard mark-to-market requirement that daily adjusts margin requirements to market conditions. Thus, if the price of the IRF increases after the two sides enter a transaction, the seller must pay the buyer the difference between the current and the IRF strike price.

IRF buyers are normally banks or investors concerned with the prospect of falling interest rates seeking to lock in a certain security yield a few weeks before they actually purchase that security (long hedge), which are usually banks holding floating income securities. IRF sellers are banks or investors concerned with the prospect of rising interest rates and security yields (short hedging), normally banks holding positions in fixed income securities.

Three-month Eurodollar interest rate futures are as follows:

Exchange	IMM (Division of the Chicago Merchantile Exchange)
Trading Hours	07.55–16.10
Size	USD 1,000,000
Symbol	E
Delivery	First business day after the last trading day
	March–June–September–December
Quotation	100 – Annual Interest Rate = Settlement Price
Tick	0.01 (1 Basis Point = USD 25); that is, 0.0001 * USD 1,000,000 * 90/360
Settlement	Cash
Delivery Date	First business day after the last trading day
Last Trading Day	11: 00—Two working days before the third Wednesday of the expiration month
Settlement Price	Based on the interest rates for the three-month Eurodollar deposits

In short, IRFs are standardized FRAs that allow banks and investors in general to hedge their interest rate risk positions, without the disadvantages of FRAs. Yet IRFs have their own disadvantages, they are subject to margin requirements that can tie up a substantial part of bank's cash, and cause loss of liquidity and income associated with the cash, which is not the case with interest rate options.

Interest Rate Options

As discussed in the previous chapters, options are rights but not obligations to enter a transaction on an underlying interest at a future date and price.

Interest rate options are rights but not obligations to exchange an asset at a predetermined price or interest rate yield. Interest rate options can be written on the spot interest rate or on the future rate of an underlying interest, and trade in the major futures options exchanges. The Eurolibor and the Gilt futures options, for instance, trade in the LIFFE, while the T-bonds and T-note option futures trade in the Chicago Mercantile Exchange (see Table 6.6).

As is the case with other options, interest rate options have a strike price, a premium, and are settled on a certain expiration date. As of the closing of November 4, 1999, for instance, the November 9600 Eurolibor futures calls had a premium of 0.49 or $4,900 per contract, while the January puts had a premium of 0.15 or $1,500 per contract (*Wall Street Journal* 1999, C10).

As is the case with futures, banks and investors holding fixed income asset positions expecting short-term interest rates to rise can buy put options on treasury bonds or notes. If interest rates are expected to rise, puts appreciate in value, off-setting the losses in the underlying interest; that is, the decline in the price of the fixed income security.

In short, off-balance sheet financial derivative products, such as FRAs, IRFs, and Interest Rate Options have broadened the choice of banks and investors in general in managing interest rate risks. Yet their use is limited to one period only, which is not the case with swaptions, caps, floors, collars, and swaps.

MANAGING MEDIUM-TERM INTEREST RATE RISK: INTEREST RATE SWAPTIONS, CAPS, FLOORS, AND COLLARS

Interest Rate Swaptions

As the term suggests, an interest rate swaption is an agreement to enter an interest rate swap at predetermined conditions at a future date.

Depending upon the position taken, swaptions can be classified into payer's and receiver's swaptions. A payer's swaption is like a put on a fixed interest rate instrument; that is, it is the right, but not the obligation to pay a fixed rate in exchange of a floating swap rate. A receiver's swaption is like a call agreement on a fixed interest rate agreement; that is, it is the right to receive a fixed interest rate in exchange of a floating swap rate.

Normally, swaptions are used to manage interest rate risk associated with fluctuations in medium-term interest rates on both sides of the bank balance sheet. Banks with a substantial part of fixed rate medium-term liabilities, for instance, expecting medium-term interest rates to fall can sell a liability receiver's swaption (see Table 6.6). Banks holding fixed income securities, or fixed rate mortgages and expecting higher medium-term interest rates can sell a payer's asset swaption (see Table 6.7).

Interest Rate Caps

A cap is an upper limit on interest rate fluctuations of a series of interest payments. Thus, caps protect their buyers from sharp and substantial interest rate increases over the life of the underlying financial position. If a bank buys a 12-percent cap on a floating

Table 6.6
Selective U.S. Treasury Futures Options

Product	First Introduced	Exchange
T-bonds	1982	CBOE
T-notes	1985	CBOE
T-bills	1986	CME
Eurodollar	1985	CME
Eurodeutschmark	--	LIFFE

Key: CBOE = Chicago Board Options Exchange;
CME = Chicago Merchantile Exchange;
LIFFE = London International Financial
Futures Exchange

liability, the bank is protected from an interest rate increase beyond 12 percent. Specifically, if interest rates rise beyond 12 percent, the cap seller pays the bank the difference between the actual interest rate and 12 percent (see Figure 6.2). If interest rates stay below 12 percent, the bank receives no payments, but it benefits from the lower rate. The calculation of the premium that the bank must pay to the seller is determined as follows:

$$CAP = [K * (IF - IS) * XD]/100$$

where

K = The size of interest rate–sensitive money flows

IF = Interest rate

IS = Cap strike

XD = Days/360 or days/365

Table 6.7
Interest-Rate Risk Management through Receiver's and Payer's Swaption

Swaption Position	Asset	Liability
Sell		
	Banks	Banks Holding
	Holding Fixed Income	Money Market
	Securities, or Fixed Rate	and Short-Maturity
	Mortgages and Expecting	CDs and Expecting
	Higher Medium-term	Interest
	Interest Rates to rise	Rates to rise
Buy		
	Banks	Banks Holding
	Holding Fixed Income	Money Market
	Securities, or Fixed Rate	and Short-Maturity
	Mortgages and Expecting	CDs and Expecting
	Higher Medium-term	Higher Medium-term
	Interest Rates	Interest Rates

Banks also sell caps to their clients, either as part of a loan package or separately. For example, on January 2, 2000, Bank A assigns a floating rate loan package to a customer under the following conditions:

Principal: $10,000,000 loan to a customer
Maturity: Three years
Interest Rate: LIBOR
Current LIBOR: 5 percent
Cap: 7 percent

Figure 6.2
Interest Rate Cap

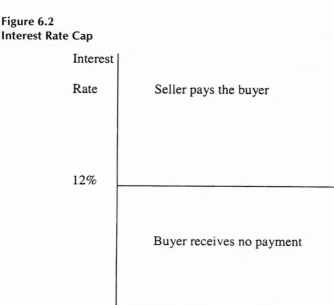

This means that the loan payments can increase or decrease along with LIBOR, but they cannot exceed 7 percent. Specifically, if LIBOR stays below 7 percent, the cap seller (the bank) makes no payment toward the borrowers loan payments (see Table 6.8), but if LIBOR exceeds the 7 percent, the bank will pay the difference. If LIBOR, for instance, reaches 8 percent, the bank will contribute $10,000 toward the borrowers payments.

Interest Rate Floors

A floor is a lower limit on interest rate fluctuations of series of interest payments. Thus, floors protect their buyers (investors with a negative medium-term interest rate gap) from sharp interest rate declines over the life of the underlying interest. If a bank buys an 8 percent floor on a floating rate paying asset, it protects itself from an interest rate decrease below 8 percent. Specifically, if interest rates fall below 8 percent, the floor seller pays the bank (see Figure 6.3). If rates stay above 8 percent, the bank receives no payment, but it benefits from the high rates.

Table 6.8
Interest Rate Cap: An Application

Time	Cap	LIBOR	Cap-LIBOR	Payment
Initial Rate	--	5%	0	0
2-1-2000				
Adjustment				
2-1-2001	7%	8%	1%	$10,000
Adjustment	7%	8.5%	1.5	$15,000

Interest Rate Collars

A collar is the combination of a cap and a floor limit on interest rate fluctuations of series of interest payments. Thus, collars protect their buyers from sharp interest rate increases or decrease over the life of the underlying interest. If a bank buys a 12-percent cap and an 8-percent floor on a floating rate–paying asset, it protects itself from an interest rate increase beyond 12 percent or below 8 percent (see Figure 6.4).

In short, caps, floors, and collars protect banks from sharp fluctuations in interest rates over the life of the underlying interest.

MANAGING LONG-TERM INTEREST RATE RISK: INTEREST RATE SWAPS

Interest rate swaps are agreements to exchange financial flows or financial positions, a fixed income flow with a floating income flow, a fixed expense flow with a floating expense flow, one asset with another asset, and one liability with another liability.

Depending on the side of the balance sheet, the swap takes place, interest rate swaps may be classified into two categories: asset swaps and liability swaps.

Liability Swaps

Liability swaps are exchanges of interest rate flows associated with liabilities. Depending upon the type of interest flows, liability

Figure 6.3
Interest Rate Floor

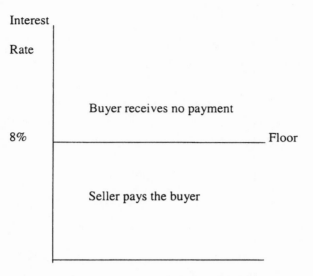

Interest

Rate

Buyer receives no payment

8%   Floor

Seller pays the buyer

Time to Maturity

swaps can be further classified in two categories: plain vanilla swaps and basis swaps.

Plain vanilla swaps are agreements between two parties to exchange payments of a floating rate loan with payments of a fixed rate loan. The party that assumes the fixed interest rate payments is taking a long position in the transaction; that is, is the swap buyer, while the party that assumes the adjustable payments is taking a short position; that is, is the seller of the swap. Plain vanilla swaps can be further classified in two categories:

1. Plain vanilla swaps in which one party has the absolute advantage in borrowing in the fixed interest rate market and the other having the absolute advantage in the variable interest rate market.
2. Plain vanilla swaps in which one party has the absolute advantage in both markets, as long as the swap is made in the market the party has the comparative advantage.

Basis plain vanilla swaps are exchanges of interest income flows on variable interest rate loans with a different basis. They can be further classified in two categories:

Figure 6.4
Interest Rate Collar

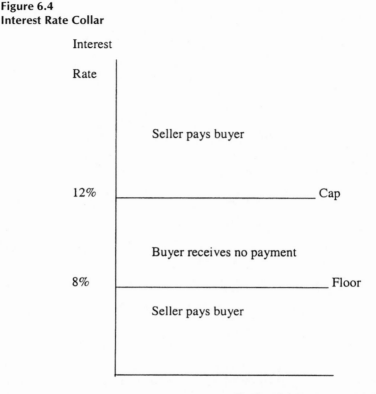

Time to Maturity

1. Absolute advantage of one side in one of the two variable interest rates.
2. Absolute advantage of one side in both types of interest rates; and the swap is made in the market in which the party has the comparative advantage.

Asset Swaps

Asset swaps are exchanges of interest rate flows associated with investments or asset claims. As was the case with liability swaps, asset swaps can be classified in two categories: plain vanilla swaps or coupon swaps, and basis swaps.

Plain vanilla swaps are agreements between two parties to exchange an adjustable investment interest payments with a fixed interest rate payments, which can be further classified in two categories:

1. Plain vanilla swaps in which one party has the absolute advantage in investing in the fixed interest rate market and the other having the absolute advantage in the variable interest rate market.
2. Plain vanilla swaps in which one party has the absolute advantage in both markets, as long as the swap is made in the market in which the party has the comparative advantage.

Basis plain vanilla swaps are exchanges of interest income flows on floating interest rate loans with a different basis. They can be further classified in two categories:

1. Absolute advantage of one side in one of the two variable interest rates.
2. Absolute advantage of one side in both interest rates, as long as the swap is made in the market in which the party has the comparative advantage.

In short, depending on the type of financial flows exchanged, interest rate swaps can be classified into liability and asset swaps, and can serve as income enhancing devices, speculative devices, and interest rate risk hedging devices, which is the focus of this section. For example, the Olympic Bank has the following financial situation:

- A combined fixed/floating rate of $100 million fixed interest rate portfolio: a fixed interest rate of 14 percent for the first five years
- Average Maturity: fifteen years
- The Olympic Bank borrowed the funds for the said loans from the interbank market LIBOR + 0.5 for the first year, and at an annually adjusted rate thereafter

Based on these data, the Olympic Bank is profitable for the first five years as long as the interest rate spread is positive; that is, LIBOR + 0.5 percent < 14 percent or LIBOR < 13.5 percent; and the lower the LIBOR, the higher the interest rate spread and the bank profit.

To protect itself against the losses associated with undesired interest rate fluctuations, the Olympic Bank enters a swap agreement, exchanging floating interest payments with fixed interest payments with a counterparty like Aegean Credit with the opposite financial situation:

- A $100,000,000 floating interest rate auto loan portfolio
- Average Maturity: five years

- Interest rate LIBOR + 0.75, renewed annually
- The funds for the said loans have been raised by issuing an 11.75 percent five-year corporate bonds

Thus, the interest rate spread and the profit or the loss of Aegean Credit depends on the variations of LIBOR:

- If LIBOR remains above 11 percent; that is, as long as (LIBOR + 0.75) > 11.75 percent or LIBOR > (11.75 percent − 0.75 percent), Aegean Credit's interest rate spread and profits are positive
- If LIBOR remains below 11 percent, Aegean Credit's interest rate and profit turn negative

The loan portfolio situation of the two institutions is summarized as follows:

Institution	Receipts	Payments
The Olympic Bank	Fixed Interest	Variable Interest
Aegean Credit	Variable Interest	Fixed Interest

The actual swap between the two institutions is summarized in Figure 6.5.

- The Olympic Bank will pay Aegean Credit a fixed interest rate of 12.1 percent for five years and will receive LIBOR.
- Payments will be based on a notional principal amount of $100 million. The notional amount is simply set for calculation purposes, not to be transferred from the one party to another.

By entering this swap both parties have reduced the variation of their interest rate spread:

The Olympic Bank

Loan Receipts	14%
Payments to Aegean Credit	12.10
Profit	1.90
Payments to the Interbank Market	LIBOR
(Cost of Capital)	LIBOR + 0.50
Loss	0.50
Total Return	1.40

Figure 6.5
The Olympic Bank and Aegean Credit Interest Rate Swap

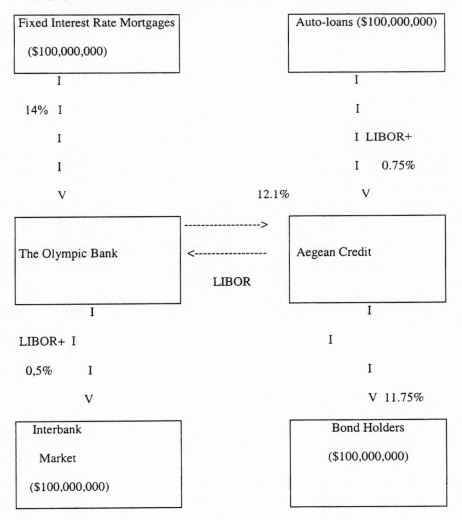

Aegean Credit

Credit Receipts	LIBOR + 0.75
Payments to the Olympic Bank	LIBOR
	———
Profit	0.75
Payments to Bondholders	12.10
(Cost of Capital)	11.75
	———
Profit	0.35
Total Return	1.1%

In short, the interest swap described in this example allows the Olympic Bank to hedge its interest rate risk position and realize gains which it must share with its counterpart, Aegean Credit. In fact, the Olympic Bank's share of the swap profit is higher than Aegean's Credit.

Now, let us assume that the swap agreement required that the Olympic Bank pay Aegean Credit 13 percent instead of 12.1 percent, and Aegean Credit pay the Olympic Bank the LIBOR rate, that is, the same as before. In that case, the Olympic Bank would earn a profit of 0.50 percent and Aegean Credit 2 percent. Thus, the total swap gain is the same as the total difference in interest rates, a matter of negotiation between the two parties.

The total gain is calculated as the sum of the fixed interest differentials; that is

14 percent − 11.75 percent = 2.25 percent

and the two variable interest rates; that is

(LIBOR + 0.75 percent) − (LIBOR + 0.5 percent) = 0.25 percent

The total difference equals 2.5 percent.

So far it is assumed that the two parties enter a swap directly with each other, which is not always the case. Swaps are made with the swap dealers, financial brokers. In that case, the earlier swap takes the form in Figure 6.6.

The dealer's profit is as follows:

Figure 6.6
The Olympic Bank and Aegean Credit Interest Rate Receipts and Payments in a Dealer Swap

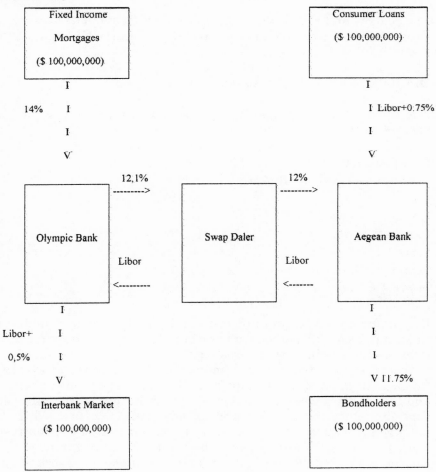

Receipts from the Olympic Bank	12.1%
Payments to Aegean Credit	12.0%
Profit	0.1%
Receipts from Aegean Credit	LIBOR
Payments to the Olympic Bank	LIBOR
Profit	0
Total Profit:	0.1%

The dealer's profit is the difference between the payments to Aegean Credit (12%) and the payments it received from the Olympic Bank (12.1%), 0.1 percent:

Drs 100,000,000 * 0.1% = 10,000

The fixed return of Aegean Credit drops to 1.0 percent, from 1.1 percent in the direct swap:

Credit Receipts	LIBOR + 0.75%
Credit Payments to the Broker	LIBOR
Profit:	0.75%
Receipts from the Broker	12.00%
Capital Cost (Bond Loan)	11.75%
Profit:	0.25%
Total Fixed Return	1.00%
(0.75% + 0.25%)	

Depending on the bargaining position of the two parties, the total "locked in" cost (2.5 percent in the example) remains the same and is to be divided among the three parties.

To sum up, interest rate risk management begins with the careful measurement of the position risk; that is, the portfolio duration and the measurement of interest income risk; that is, the interest rate gap. Once the position and income risk are measured, risk management advances to the next stage, the hedging of interest sensitive balance sheet positions by the entrance of financial derivative contracts that mitigate losses in the underlying securities.

Hedging of interest rate risk with financial derivatives must be jointly applied with traditional methods in the management of interest rate risk, and their choice-mix must reflect the institution's overall policy objectives and cost considerations, which is also the case for foreign exchange risk management discussed in the next chapter.

NOTES

1. In a narrow sense, immunization is a technique that equalizes the duration of a security with the investor's holding period. In a broader sense, immunization is a technique that neutralizes the effect of interest rates on the bank's balance sheet. For details, see Gup (1984).

2. As discussed in the previous chapters, the use of a particular risk management method depends on the overall management objectives. If the objective of the bank is to hedge risks rather than to enchance income, management can just hedge a balance sheet position by taking an offsetting off-balance sheet position: for example, offsetting a long balancesheet position with a short off-balance sheet position. In this case, the bank does not need to forecast the direction of interest rates.

7

Foreign Exchange
Risk Management

In the late 1990s, as Greece was preparing to join the European
Monetary Union (EMU), Olympic Bank economists had yet another
worry, the prospect of a Greek Drachma devaluation against major
European currencies, especially against the Deutchmark (DM). If
materialized, such a currency devaluation would have an adverse
effect on standby lending commitments to Greek importers.

In a deregulated global economy where funds cross national bor-
ders at a mouse click, Olympic Bank is not alone. American and
European banks, which borrowed in Japanese yen to take advantage of the large interest rate differentials between their own domestic and Japanese interest rates also faced the foreign exchange
rate risk. As discussed in the previous chapters, every bank that
draws part of its liabilities from, or allocates part of its investment
or loan portfolio to foreign markets is exposed to foreign exchange
risk, especially banks expanding their operations in countries with
highly volatile currencies, as is the case with emerging economies.

Banks are not the only institutions concerned with foreign exchange risk. So are the world's large corporations that are engaged
in international trade and investments.

The company hedges the exposure of accounts receivable and a portion of anticipated foreign currency fluctuations, primarily with options contracts. The Company monitors its foreign currency exposure daily to ensure the overall effectiveness of its foreign currency hedge positions. Principal hedges include the Japanese yen, British pound, German mark, French franc, and Canadian dollar. Fixed income securities are subject to interest rate risk. The Company routinely hedges its exposure to interest rate risk with options in case of a catastrophic increase in interest rates. (Microsoft Annual Report 1999, 25)

The Company conducts business on a global basis in several major international currencies. As such, it is exposed to adverse movements in foreign currency exchange rates. The Company enters into forward foreign exchange contracts to reduce certain currency exposures. (Cisco Systems Annual Report 1999, 46)

How can banks, multinational corporations, and investors in general protect their net income and net worth against the foreign currency risk?

As was the case with the interest rate risk, to protect themselves against foreign currency risks, banks must first calculate their net exposure to each currency (FX gap) as discussed in Chapter 3, then apply conventional, on-balance sheet and modern off-balance sheet methods to control them. A conventional foreign exchange risk management method, for instance, is the restructuring of foreign currency denominated assets and liabilities, so as to immunize or insulate the balance sheet from foreign currency fluctuations. Greek banks with a positive DM currency gap expecting a DM appreciation, for instance, can issue DM denominated CDs to offset their position.

A modern method is to enter financial derivative contracts. Banks with an FX gap expecting a depreciation of the domestic currency can buy FX futures or FX futures calls. Conversely, banks with an FX gap expecting the domestic currency to appreciate can sell FX futures or buy FX puts.

As was the case with interest rate gaps, the choice depends on the expected time horizon of the foreign exchange appreciation or depreciation. Banks, for instance, concerned with short-term currency fluctuations can enter Forward Foreign Currency Contracts (FFCC), FX futures, and FX options, while banks concerned with long-term foreign currency fluctuations can enter FX swaps.

As of June 1998, foreign exchange derivative contracts have reached a notional amount of $22,055 billion and a market value of $982 billion. The largest position was in outright forward and forex derivatives amounting to a notional amount of $14,658 billion and

Table 7.1
Global Positions in OTC Foreign Exchange Derivative
Contracts as of June 1998 (Billions of U.S. Dollars)

	Notional Amounts	Gross Market Values
Outright forward and Forex	14,658	584
Currency Swaps	2,324	255
Options	5,040	141
Other	33	2
Total	22,055	982

Source: Bank of International Settlements (1999), p. 23.

a market value of $584 billion, followed by currency swaps and currency options (see Table 7.1).

Addressing modern foreign currency risk management methods in more detail, this chapter is in two sections. The first section discusses the management of FX risk due to short-term currency fluctuations with FFCC, FX futures, and FX options. The second section discusses the FX management of risk due to long-term foreign currency fluctuations with foreign currency swaps.

SHORT-TERM CURRENCY FLUCTUATIONS: FORWARD FOREIGN CURRENCY CONTRACTS, FUTURES, AND OPTIONS

Forward Foreign Currency Contracts (FFCC)

Forward Foreign Currency Contracts are contracts that oblige two parties to exchange a foreign currency at a predetermined rate at a future time. FFCC allows the two parties to hedge their positions against future foreign currency fluctuations; that is, buyers protect themselves against a currency appreciation, and sellers protect themselves against a currency depreciation. For example, when a U.S. bank buys German government fixed-income securities, it faces foreign currency risk. Should the mark depreciate against the dollar, the bank will realize losses when the fixed income position is liquidated and the marks are converted to dollars. Should the mark appreciate against the dollar, the bank will realize gains when marks are converted to dollars.

The bank can hedge its German securities position, by applying both on-balance sheet and off-balance sheet methods. On-balance methods include the taking of a liability position in Deutchmarks, for instance, by issuing of mark-denominated CDs. Fluctuations on the asset side of the balance sheet are exactly offset by fluctuations on the liability side of the balance sheet (see Figure 7.1). Off-balance methods include the purchase of forward mark contracts that would allow the bank to buy marks, say nine months from now (if that is the length of time the bank plans to hold the German securities), at a fixed exchange rate set today, say, $0.60 per mark.

The most important element of a FFCC is the Forward Exchange Rate (FWD) that eliminates differences in investment returns across different currencies and therefore leaves the two parties indifferent regarding the currency denomination of their positions.

The Forward Exchange Rate (FWD) is determined by a number of the same factors that determine Spot Exchange Rates (SPOT), such as the trade balance, expectations, and economic conditions. Yet due to the difference in nominal interest rates in different countries, FWD is in general different than spot exchange rates.

The theoretical value of the FWD can be calculated by the following formula:

$$FWD = SPOT * \frac{1 + IL * T}{1 + IF * T}$$

where

IL = Domestic currency interest rate

IF = Foreign currency exchange rate

T = time (If time is less than the discount period, it is expressed in days; that is, as a discount period, T= D/360).

To illustrate the difference between spot and FWD, consider a Greek bank that has raised funds by issuing a 4-percent DM100,000 three-month CD. To enhance its profit, the bank has two options:

Figure 7.1
Hedging a Short Position with FX Forward Contracts

Currency Gains/Losses (%)

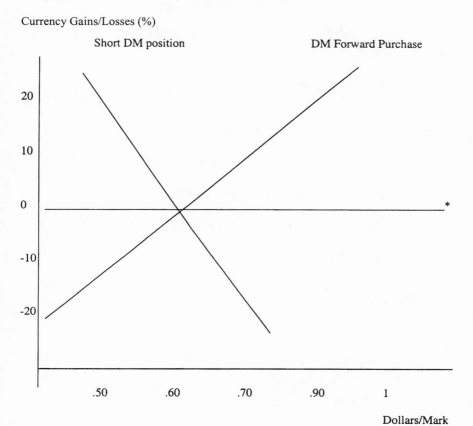

*Hedging result

First, extend a three-month DM-denominated loan. Second, convert DM into drachmas and extend a drachma loan, and three months later when the CD matures, return the DM to the depositors. Which choice is better?

It depends on the interest rate differentials and the drachma/DM exchange rate at the time of the initial conversion of DM to Drachmas and the subsequent conversion of drachmas to DM. Assuming that at the time of the initial conversion, the Greek drachma-denominated CDs pay a 16-percent interest, and the spot exchange is 160 drachma per DM.

The DM-denominated loan yields the following:

DM 100.000 * 0.04 * 90/360 = DM 1,000

Principal + Interest = DM 101,000

If he converts his DM to drachmas at the spot rate, his drachma principle will be the following:

DM 100,000 * 160 = DM 16,000,000
(or DM 100,000 / 0.00625)

In this case, the return is as follows:

DR 16,000,000 * 0.16 * 90/360 = DR 640,000

Principal + Interest = DR 16,640,000

Based on these data, the forward exchange rate (FWD), the exchange rate that equilizes currency denominated returns, can be calculated as follows:

$$\text{FWD} = \frac{\text{DM } 16,640,000}{\text{DM } 101,000} = \text{DR } 164,752$$

or

$$\frac{\text{DM } 101.000}{\text{DR } 16,640,000} = \text{DM } 0.006069$$

If at the end of the three-month period, the bank had converted drachmas to DM at a rate of DM/DR 164.752 or DR/DM 0.006069, its return would not have been affected by currency fluctuations:

DR 16,640,000 / 164.752 = DM 101,000 (or 16,640,000/1.04),

that is the same as in DM, or

DM 101,000 * 164.752 = DR 16,640,000,

the same as if the investment was in DR.

The decision to invest in DM or DR assets depends on FWD. If the exchange rate was below DM/DR 164.752, the drachma-denominated investment would have had a higher return. By contrast, if the exchange rate was higher than 164.752, the DM-denominated investment would have had a higher return.

$$FWD = 160 * \frac{1+ 0.16 * \dfrac{90}{360}}{1 + 0.04 * \dfrac{90}{360}} = 160 * 1.024703 = 164.752$$

FWD = 251.698

and

Swap Rate = 21.698

In short, FWD, the exchange rate that eliminates the foreign exchange risk and the interest rate arbitrage for the two currencies is determined by the interest rate differentials of the two currencies. It is the basis for the foreign currency derivatives.

Moreover, the difference between the forward and the spot rate is the swap rate; that is, the interest rate differentials. Formally,

Swap Rate = Forward Exchange Rate − Spot Rate

Conversely,

Forward Exchange Rate = Spot Rate + Swap Rate

The Swap Rate is calculated as follows:

$$\text{Swap Rate} = \text{Spot} * \left[\frac{1 + IL * T}{1 + IF * T} \right] - \text{Spot}$$

where

IL = Domestic interest rates

IF = Foreign interest rates

Thus the swap rate also depends on interest rate differentials. The larger the interest rate differentials, the larger the divergence between forward and spot exchange.

Applying the data of the previous example, the swap rate can be calculated as follows:

$$\text{Swap Rate} = 160 * \left[\frac{1 + 0.16 * (90/360)}{1 + 0.04 * (90/360)} \right] - 160 = 4.752$$

If the forward rate is below the spot rate, that is, if the swap rate is negative, the currency sells at a discount. Conversely, if the forward rate is above the spot rate, the domestic currency sells at a premium:

$$\text{FD or FP} = \frac{\text{FR} - \text{SR}}{\text{SR}}$$

where

FD = Forward Discount

FP = Forward Premium

FR = Forward Rate

SR = Spot Rate

Applying this formula where the spot rate is 160 and the forward rate is 150, as in the earlier example, the DM sells at a forward discount of 10 DR or 6.25 for the three-month period or 25 percent on an annual basis:

FD = [(DR 150 − DR 160)/(DR 160)] * 4 * 100
   = − 25% (Forward Discount)

Discount/Premium Bid Rate

Given the difference between spot and forward rate, the Discount or Premium bid and offered swap rate can be calculated as follows:

$$\text{D/P Bid Rate} = \frac{\text{SPOT bid} * (\text{LC bid} - \text{FC offered}) * \text{D}}{360 * 100 + (\text{FC offered} * \text{D})}$$

$$\text{D/P Offered Rate} = \frac{\text{SPOT offered} * (\text{LC offered} - \text{FC bid}) * \text{D}}{360 * 100 + (\text{FC bid} * \text{D})}$$

where:

SPOT bid = Spot rate bid (purchase)

SPOT offered = Spot rate offered (sale)

LC bid = Interest rate bid (deposit) of domestic currency

LC offered = Interest rate offered (lending) of domestic currency

FC bid = Interest rate bid (lending) of foreign currency

FC offered = Interest rate offered (lending) of foreign currency

D = Time period (days)

For example:

- Domestic currency = DM
- Foreign currency = $
- Spot rate $/DM 1.610 (bid)
- Spot rate $/DM 1.630 (offered)
- Annual interest of six-month Eurodeposits $ 5.30 percent (bid)
- Annual interest of six-month Eurodeposits $ 5.55 percent (offered)
- Annual interest of six-month Eurodeposits DM 3.50 percent (bid)
- Annual interest of six-month Eurodeposits DM 3.75 percent (offered)
- D = 180

Based on this formula, the D/P Bid Rate is as follows:

$$\text{D/P Bid Rate} = \frac{\text{SPOT bid} * (\text{DM bid} - \$ \text{ offered}) * \text{D}}{360 * 100 + (\$ \text{ offered} * \text{D})}$$

$$= \frac{1.610 * (3.50 - 5.55) * 180}{360 * 100 + (5.55 * 180)}$$

$$= -0.0160569$$

This figure provides the difference between the current and the forward rates of the two currencies. It is a negative number because the forward rate of the dollar is selling at a discount to the spot rate, which suggests that the swap participants expect the dollar to fall against the DM in the said period.

Specifically, the six-month forward rate is determined as follows:

FRD bid = Spot − Discount
      = 1.61000 − 0.0160569
      = 1.5994 DM per Dollar

The expected fall of the dollar reflects the interest rate differential between the two countries.

Foreign Currency Futures

As discussed in the previous chapters, foreign currency futures are standardized agreements between two parties to exchange an underlying foreign currency at a predetermined rate at a future date.

As standardized products, foreign exchange futures contracts trade on organized exchanges, which also determine their size, trade, and delivery conditions. The Japanese yen, the Canadian dollar, the British pound, and the Swiss franc, for instance, all trade on the Chicago Mercantile Exchange (see Table 7.2).

Foreign exchange futures are also subject to a number of government regulations, such as margin requirements, which are monitored daily by futures exchanges, and adjusted to market fluctuations, as explained in the following example.

At the beginning of the trading day on November 1, the Greek drachma traded at 300 drachmas to the dollar. Two banks, the Olympic Bank, seeking to hedge its FX portfolio against a stronger dollar, and the Athenian Bank, seeking to hedge its FX position against a weaker dollar, enter an FX contract; the Olympic Bank is the buyer, and the Athenian Bank is the seller.

Assuming further that the size of the contract is $100,000, the initial required margin is 5 percent and the required margin is 3 percent, the subsequent (maintenance) margin is 3 percent.

Table 7.2
Selective FX Futures

Product	Exchange	Size
Japanese Yen	CME	$12.5 million
Canadian Dollar	CME	CA $100,000
British Pound	CME	62,500,000 pounds
Swiss Franc	CME	125,000 francs

The initial margin to be deposited in the futures account is DR 3,000,000; that is (100,000 * 300 * 2) * 5 percent, while the maintenance margin is DR 2,100,000; that is (100,000 * 300* 2) * 3.5 percent. The notional amount of the two contracts is DR 60,000,000 or $200,000. Given the 3-percent maintenance margin, the mark-to-market positions for different drachma/dollar exchange rates given in Tables 7.3 and 7.4.

Olympic Bank's (Buyer's) Margin Account

The transaction begins with an order placed by the buyer on September 1 to purchase two 300 U.S. dollar futures contracts.[1] The buyer is required to deposit an initial margin of DR 3,000,000. The order is executed and the buyer holds two $100,000 contracts, a total value of $200,000.

At the end of the first day, the Greek currency appreciated by two drachmas against the dollar, that is, 298DR/$. Thus, the investor incurred a loss of DR 400,000 ($200,000 * 2), which requires an adjustment, a marking of his margin account to the market conditions. Specifically, the buyer's margin account should be charged DR 400,000, which will be transferred to the sellers account. Thus, a new contract is in effect with a new exchange rate DR298/$. This procedure is repeated every trade day, until the settlement day. In this sense, futures contracts could be seen as successive contracts reflecting the changing market conditions (see Table 7.3).

Mark-to-market is repeated after the closing of the second and third days' transactions, when the dollar continues to fall against

Table 7.3
Margin Account and the Marking-to-Market (Buyer–Long Position)

Date	Future Price	Daily Profit/Loss	Cumulative Profit/Loss	Margin Balance
	300			3,000,000
1/9	298	(400,000)	(400,000)	2,600,000
2/9	297	(200,000)	(600,000)	2,400,000
3/9	295.5	(300,000)	(900,000)	2,100,000
4/9	297.5	400,000	(500,000)	2,500,000
5/9	296	(300,000)	(800,000)	2,200,000
6/9	294	(400,000)	(1,200,000)	1,800,000
				+1,200,000
				3,000,000
7/9	293	(200,000)	(1,400,000)	2,800,000
8/9	295	400,000	(1,000,000)	3,200,000
				-200,000
				3,000,000
9/9	292	(600,000)	(1,600,000)	2,400,000
10/9	290	(400,000)	(2,000,000)	2,000,000
				+1,000,000
				3,000,000
11/9	289	(200,000)	(2,200,000)	2,800,000
12/9	287	(400,000)	(2,600,000)	2,400,000

Table 7.4
Margin Account and the Marking-to-Market (Seller–Short Position)

Date	Future Price	Daily Profit/Loss	Cumulative Profit/Loss	Margin Balance
	300			3,000.000
1/9	298	400,000	400,000	3,400.000
2/9	297	200,000	600,000	3,600.000
3/9	295.5	300,000	900,000	3,900.000
4/9	297.5	(400,000)	500,000	3,500.000
5/9	296	300,000	800,000	3,800.000
6/9	294	400,000	1,200,000	4,100.000
7/9	293	200,000	1,400,000	4,300.000
8/9	295	(400,000)	1,000,000	3,900.000
9/9	292	600,000	1,600,000	4,500.000
10/9	290	400,000	2,000,000	4,900.000
11/9	289	200,000	2,200,000	5,100.000
12/9	287	400,000	2,600,000	5,600.000

the drachma. The total loss for the investor appears in the fourth column and has reached DR 900,000, driving the account balance down to DR 2,100,000.

The next day, the market conditions reverse themselves, and the dollar rises two drachmas, resulting in a DR 400,000 profit and driving total losses down to DR 500,000. The buyer's account is credited by transferring the said amount from the seller's account. In the following days, the dollar reverses course, resuming its decline against the drachma, and the buyer continues to accumulate losses, while the seller accumulates gains, until on September 6 its margin balance reaches DR 1,800,000. At this point, the buyer receives a "margin call," requiring an additional deposit of 1,200,000, so as his balance may return to DR 3,000,000, which is the margin requirement. On September 10, the dollar continues to fall against the drachma and the buyer is called to add another DR 1,000,000 to his margin account.[2]

On the contract expiration date, September 12, the dollar drops against the drachma. Thus, as it is indicated from the fourth column, the buyer realized a final loss of 2,600,000. The same day, the contract seller must deliver the contract buyer the underlying interest; that is, $200,000 in exchange for 57,400,000, or (2 * 100.000) * 287.

Athenian Bank's (Seller's) Margin Account

Futures trading is a zero-sum game. One side's losses are the other side's gains. Thus, any time the contract buyer's account is charged with a loss, the seller's account is credited with a gain of exactly the same amount (see Table 7.4).

The numbers in the table assume that the contract seller is subjected to a 3-percent margin requirement. Needless to say, since the seller realizes gains he or she does not deposit any additional reserves into his or her account. Nevertheless, it is assumed that the gains, which amount to DR 2,600,000 remain in the account.

In short, FX futures are standardized products that allow banks and investors in general to hedge their net worth position and net income flows against foreign currency fluctuations. As standardized products trading in major exchanges, FX futures provide buyers and sellers with a number of advantages, such as liquidity and prompt execution, while minimizing the probability of seller's default. Yet they require the deposit of margin funds, a drag to the bank's liquidity and interest rate income, which is not the case with FX options.

Foreign Currency Options

As discussed in the previous chapters, options are contracts that provide their holders the right but not the obligation to buy an underlying interest at a predetermined price for a specified period of time. Foreign currency options provide their holders the right to buy or sell a currency at a prespecified (strike) price (exchange rate). The price is written in another currency. The currency whose units are used for the premium and the strike price to be assigned is called trading currency. The currency to be bought or sold is the underlying currency.

As with options contracts in general, foreign exchange options trade on major options exchanges and are classified as Call Options and Put Options. Foreign exchange calls allow their buyers to hedge their short currency positions against a foreign currency appreciation, while foreign currency puts allow their holders to hedge their long currency positions against a foreign currency depreciation.

To understand how options work, the following example compares and contrasts the profits and losses associated with two options contracts, a call and a put contract with the same strike price and the same expiration date, held by the same investor, a strategy known as currency straddle. For example, take the gains and losses from a currency straddle.

Consider two foreign currency options with the following characteristics:

Foreign currency = U.S. dollar ($)

Underlying interest = Greek drachma (DR)

Call strike price = 300 DR/$

Put strike price = 300 DR/$

Premium = 22 DR

Contract size = $100,000

Total premium = 2,200,000 DR

Life = three months

Given these contract characteristics, the profits and the losses from the two positions depend on the DR/$ exchange rate values during the life of the contracts, as indicated in Table 7.5.

In short, FX currency options provide for a relatively inexpensive hedge against short-term currency fluctuations.

Table 7.5
Profits and Losses for the Straddle Holder (Thousands of Drachmas)

Exchange Rate*	Profit or Loss		STRADDLE
	CALL (HOLDER)	PUT (HOLDER)	
240	-2.200	+3.800	+1.600
250	-2.200	+2.800	+ 600
260	-2.200	+1.800	- 600
270	-2.200	+ 800	- 1.400
278	-2.200	0	-. 2.200
280	-2.200	-200	- 2.400
290	-2.200	-1.200	- 3.400
295	-2.200	-1.700	- 3.900
300	-2.200	-2.200	- 4.400
305	-1.700	-2.200	-3.900
310	-1.200	-2.200	-3.400
320	- 200	-2.200	-2.400
322	0	-2.200	-2.200
330	+ 800	-2.200	-1.400
340	+1.800	-2.200	- 400
350	+2.800	-2.200	+ 600
360	+3.800	-2.200	+ 1.600

*DR/$

LONG-TERM FOREIGN CURRENCY FLUCTUATIONS:
FOREIGN CURRENCY SWAPS

Currency swaps are agreements between two parties for the exchange of different currencies or currency-denominated payment flows at prespecified prices. Currency swaps include three stages:

1. Principal Swap—the purchase or sale of one currency against another in spot prices.
2. Exchange of Financial Flows—the exchange of interest income flows while the agreement is in effect.
3. Principal Swap—the return of the principal.

To understand how swaps work, consider two Greek banks, Bank A and Bank B, with the following FX positions.

Bank A:

· has borrowed from a U.S. bank $10,000 for one year at 6 percent.
· The loan is to be paid at the end of the year.
· The current exchange rate is 230 drachma/$.

Bank B:

· has borrowed from the domestic Greek market 2,300,000 drachmas ($10,000) for one year at 16 percent.
· The loan is to be paid at the end of the year.

Since the principal of the loan will be converted in drachmas at the beginning of the loan period and the loan payment will be converted back to dollars at the end of the period, Bank A is exposed to foreign exchange risk. A depreciation of the drachma against the dollar will result in substantial currency losses. Conversely, an appreciation of drachma against the dollar will result in substantial currency gains.

To hedge its position against foreign exchange risk, Bank A can enter a foreign currency swap with Bank B in three stages:

1. Bank A exchanges with Bank B $10,000 for DR 2,300,000 ($10,000 * DR 230).
2. At the end of the year, Bank A exchanges the interest income of DR 368,000 (DR 2,300,000 * 16%) with Bank B and receives $600 ($10,000 * 6%).

3. At the end of the year, the two companies exchange the original loan principals; that is, Bank A delivers Bank B DR 2,300,000 and receives $10,000, which applies toward the repayment of the dollar-denominated loan.

The financial flows of the swap for Bank A are illustrated in detail in Figure 7.2 and Table 7.6.

Note that the principal drachma and dollar values exchanged at the end of the year are the same as those exchanged in the beginning of the period; that is, DR 2,300,000 for $10,000, irrespective of the exchange at that day. Thus, the exchange funds are not affected by currency fluctuations at the end of the period.

The reason the exchanged principals remain the same at the beginning and at the end of the swap period is because the difference in the currency between the beginning and the end of the period is determined only by the interest rate differential, as discussed earlier. Specifically, while at the beginning of the period the exchange rate was 230 DR/$, at the end of the period it was as follows:

$$FWD = SPOT * (1 + IL * T/1 + IF * T)$$

where

FWD = Forward exchange rate

$SPOT$ = Current exchange rate

IL = Domestic interest rates (DR)

IF = Foreign interest rates ($)

T = Time (if less than a 360-day year, ($T = D/360$)

To sum up, modern FX risk management begins with the careful measurement of FX gap, and continues with the application of on- and off-balance sheet policies to reduce or even eliminate it. On-balance sheet policies restructure foreign currency-denominated asset and liability positions, so as to immunize the balance sheet from anticipated FX fluctuations. Off-balance sheet policies apply financial derivatives, such as FX futures, FX options, and FX swaps to hedge foreign currency asset and liability positions.

Figure 7.2
Currency Swap between Banks A and B

a) Foreign Currency Loan

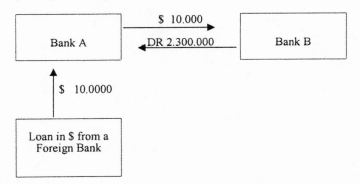

b) Interest Rate Swap

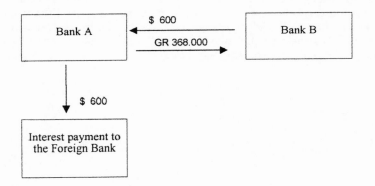

c) Exchange of Principal

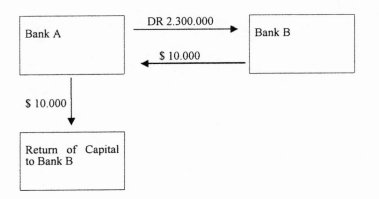

Table 7.6
Receipts and Payments in a Foreign Currency Swap (Bank A)

Receipts	Payments
DR2,300,000	$10,000
$600	DR368,000
$10,000	DR2,300,00

NOTES

1. Here, it is assumed that drachma futures trade on an organized futures exchange.

2. At this point, one may raise the question: What would have happened, should the buyer has failed to meet "margin calls"; that is, deposit the additional funds to meet margin requirements? The brokerage firm would have had to liquidate his account. Thus, the mark-to-market process minimizes the risk that one side may suffer excessive losses and fail to meet its obligations to the other side.

8

Conclusion

Financial markets operate efficiently only when participants can commit to transactions with reasonable confidence that the risk of nonpayment can be rationally judged and compensated for. Fear, whether irrational or otherwise, grips participants and they unthinkingly disengage from risky assets in favor of those providing safety and liquidity. The subtle distinctions that investors make, so critical to the effective operation of financial markets, are abandoned. Assets, good and bad, are dumped indiscriminately in circumstances of high uncertainty and fear that are not conducive to planning and investment.

Alan Greenspan (1998, 2)

History teaches that in the financial markets there will come a day unlike any other day. The leverage that once multiplied income will now devastate principal.

Martin Mayer (1999, 2)

Risk, as an act of God, a matter of poor judgment, or as the outcome of reckless behavior, has always been a factor to reckon with in everyday life and in the business community. Corporations, small and large, have always been exposed to the whims of nature, technology, and legislation that disrupt their operations and devastate their performance. Corporations have also been exposed to the forces of competition and the erratic commodity and resource price movements that create winners and losers.

For years, government protectionism and regulation and information inefficiencies sheltered domestic and local industries from outside competition and from currency and interest rate fluctuations and the risks associated with them. This was especially true for the financial service industry and the banking industry in particular, which maintained a steady corporate clientele and enjoyed a number of favorable central banking and government policies: the service of the central bank discount window, government subsidization and bailing out of their corporate clients, and government mandates that required banks to invest a substantial part of their deposits in low-risk government securities.

In such a highly protected environment, risk was a minor factor in bank management handled intuitively by career bureaucrats and credit officers. Banking was a passive and routine financial intermediation process, the amassing of deposits and the dispensing of loans and credit. This was especially the case in the first three decades that followed the end of World War II, when robust economic growth and a positive interest rate spread allowed the banking industry to grow and prosper through seigniorage income alone. The job of bank managers was similar to that of river gatekeepers who monitor the stream flow through the gate, diverting a portion of the stream to the bank treasury.

In recent years, trade liberalization, government deregulation, and the spread of information technology have eliminated market sanctuaries, creating new business opportunities and exposing corporations to the whim of market forces. For the banking industry in particular, government deregulation and the spread of new technology have lowered geographical boundaries, allowing banks to expand their traditional activities to achieve economies of scale. Government deregulation and new technology have further lowered the industry boundaries, allowing banks to expand to the other segments of the financial services industry and to offer new products and services to a larger and more diverse clientele.

At the same time, banks have been exposed to rising risks arising from both the intensification of competition across geographical and industry boundaries and the liberalization of interest rates and foreign currency rates. Risk is no longer just an act of God, poor judgment or reckless behavior, but the inevitable consequence of the intensification of international, domestic, and local competition, and a major factor in bank management. Banking is being transformed from a passive and routine financial intermediation process into an active and dynamic risk management process handled by mathematicians and rocket scientists.

Accommodating the transformation of the banking industry from a financial intermediary to a risk manager are two separate developments. First, the development of modern risk measurement techniques, such as duration, gap analysis, and value at risk that allowed banks to accurately measure and monitor market risks. Second, financial reengineering, the development of financial products that allowed banks to hedge risk exposure. FRAs, T-bond futures, T-bond futures options, and interest rate swaps allow banks to hedge their positions against interest rate risk, while foreign currency futures and options, and foreign currency swaps allow banks to hedge their foreign currency risks.

An overview of banking risks and their management, this book took a close look at the philosophical and operational approaches to banking risk management; the evolution of banking risk management under both the multinational and the global economy; the off-balance sheet risk management methods; and the use of on- and off-balance sheet methods to manage three core banking risks: credit risk, interest rate risk, and foreign exchange risk.

Arguing that risk management is both a philosophical and an operational concept, Chapter 2 was in two sections. The first section began with the distinction among the three different attitudes toward risk—risk attraction, risk neutrality, risk aversion—and the ways they shape risk management strategies. The second section continued with the identification of banking risks, which were classified risks in two major categories:

1. Traditional banking risks; that is, risks stemming from the basic function of banks as intermediaries, which were further classified in four categories, liquidity risk, credit risk, political and legal risk, and operations risk.
2. Nontraditional banking risks are risks associated with the liberalization of foreign exchange and domestic financial markets, the domestic and overseas expansion of banks and their venturing to the other segments of the financial service industry. Nontraditional risks include market risks and other risks. Market risks include interest rate risk, while other risks include commodity risk, financial investment risk, and financial derivatives risk.

The section further discussed individual risk measures that measure the separate impact of each risk on a bank's performance, and aggregate risk measures that measure the comprehensive impact of all types of risks on bank performance. Individual measures of interest rate risk include duration, gap analysis, and convexity. Individual measures of foreign exchange rate risk include FX sensitivity or gap analysis. Individual measures of credit risk include ratio analysis, while individual investment risk measures include the mean variance model, and the capital asset pricing model. Aggregate risk measures include VAR and total risk models.

The section ended with an overview of risk monitoring and control methods. Particular emphasis was placed on the distinction between on-balance sheet and off-balance sheet methods. On-balance sheet methods focus on the restructuring of assets and liabilities to immunize the balance sheet against interest rate and foreign exchange rate fluctuations. Off-balance sheet methods focus on hedging interest and FX sensitive bank positions against such fluctuations.

Chapter 3 argued that banking risk management is an ever-changing process, adapting to changes in the market environment and industry structure. In the first three-quarters of the twentieth century, banking risk management was an on-balance sheet operation, focusing on the two traditional risks, liquidity and credit risk. Liquidity risk was managed with sound accounting, shortening the maturity of assets, extending the maturity of liabilities, and maintaining close relations with other banks and central bankers. Credit risk was primarily managed by relational banking; that is, by the development of close relations with customers, and by carefully monitoring and measuring their credit worthiness; and by investing in low-risk government securities. In the last quarter of the twentieth century, banking risk management expanded to off-balance sheet operations, focusing on the management of market risks, and most notably on the interest rate and foreign exchange risk with the use of financial derivatives.

Chapter 4 reviewed the characteristics of financial derivative products, emphasizing their advantages and disadvantages as off-balance sheet risk management devices. As over the counter products, forward contracts cater to specialized short-term risk management needs that are not covered by organized markets and are premium free. As standardized products, futures contracts normally cater to short-term general risk management needs; trade on organized exchanges; and are premium free. Options also cater to the general risk management needs; trade on organized exchanges; and bear a premium. As over the counter products, swaps also cater to specialized risk management needs, do not trade on organized exchanges, and do not bear a premium. Caps, floors, collars, and swaptions normally cater to specialized medium-term risk management needs; they do not trade on organized exchanges; and bear a premium.

The chapter further discussed the suitability of each instrument in the management of banking risks. Banks expecting short- or medium-term interest rate fluctuations can enter FRA agreements and participate in the Eurodollar futures and option markets. Banks expecting a foreign currency appreciation can buy foreign currency futures and options of that currency. The chapter ended with a discussion of the problems that arise when financial derivatives are used as speculative devices.

Addressing credit risk management in more detail, Chapter 5 was in two sections. The first section was a review of a conventional credit scoring and ranking, which includes five stages. The first stage consists of the collection of quantitative and qualitative information about the financial situation of their current and prospective clients. The second stage consists of the organization of such information in categories and the assignment of a grade to each category. The third stage derives the average total grade for all categories that classified each client into a risk class, and sets the loan terms and conditions for each risk class. The fourth stage consists of the assignment of the loan terms and conditions. Clients in low-risk classes were assigned low interest rate risk premia, while clients in high-risk classes were assigned high interest rate risk premia or their loan or credit extension application (existing clients) was rejected altogether. The fifth stage includes the close monitoring of loans, the development of historical loan probability defaults for each client category, and the adjustment of scoring and ranking systems accordingly.

The second section was a discussion of two modern, off-balance sheet credit risk management methods—credit options and credit swaps—that transfer credit risk to third parties and therefore supplement conventional credit risk management methods. Credit options and credit swaps are particularly important credit risk management tools to banks expanding in emerging economies where financial and economic information is limited and of poor quality, therefore, conventional scoring and ranking cannot be reliable.

Chapter 6 discussed in more detail the management of interest rate risks. The chapter began by reemphasizing the importance of careful measurement of position risk; that is, portfolio duration and the measurement of interest income risk, or the interest rate gap. The chapter continued with the discussion of conventional on-balance sheet methods to immunize or minimize the averse impact of rising interest rates, and even enhance a bank's net income. One such measure is the shortening of the duration of its asset portfolio and lengthening of the duration of its liabilities in the prospect of rising interest rates. Another measure is the lengthening of the duration of its asset portfolio and the shortening of bank liabilities in the prospect of lower interest rates.

The chapter further discussed the use of off-balance sheet methods to shift the interest rate risk to third parties, such as treasury bond futures, caps, floors, swaps, and so on. For banks holding long positions on fixed interest rate loans and investments, taking short treasury bond futures positions shifts the interest rate risk to the sellers of these derivative products. Likewise, for banks holding long positions on floating interest rate assets, the purchase of interest rate floors transfers interest rate risk to the sellers of these products.

Chapter 7 discussed in more detail the management of foreign currency risk. The chapter began by reemphasizing the importance of careful measurement of the FX gap, and continued with the discussion of on- and off-balance sheet policies to reduce or even eliminate it. On-balance sheet measures include the restructuring of foreign currency-denominated assets and liabilities to insulate the balance sheet from foreign currency fluctuations. Off-balance sheet policies include the use of financial derivatives, such as FX futures, FX options, and FX swaps to hedge foreign currency positions. Banks with an FX gap expecting a depreciation of the domestic currency can buy FX futures or FX futures calls. Conversely, banks with an FX gap expecting the domestic currency to appreciate, can sell FX futures or buy FX puts. The choice depends on the expected time horizon of the foreign exchange appreciation or depreciation. Banks concerned with short-term currency fluctuations can enter forward foreign currency contracts, FX futures, and FX options, while banks concerned with long-term foreign currency fluctuations can enter FX swaps.

Looking into the future, five trends will influence banking risk management. First, with the euro emerging as the new currency of EU and the elimination of FX risk in this region, FX risk management will focus on bank transactions carried in other world regions, especially in emerging markets with unstable currencies. Second, the use of off-balance risk management methods in the management of investment risk and credit risk is expected to accelerate and extend to the management of liquidity risk. Third, the growing use of off-balance risk management methods, and most notably the use of over-the-counter financial derivative products will require the better measuring, monitoring, and control of counterpart risk. Fourth, with the growing use of technology and logistics, banking risk management will become more process-oriented and less dependent on people, especially the management of market risks. Fifth, banks will expand their role as financial derivative dealers, providing to their customers bundles of traditional financial products and financial derivative products, floating rate loans and interest rate caps, floating deposits and interest rate floors, and fixed income securities and interest rate puts.

In short, banking risk management will continue to grow from a minor to a major factor in banking management, turning from a "defensive weapon to an important part of the offense," to use Meadows's and McClave's words (1996, 1). This means that the bankers must set aside the resources to acquire and use this weapon efficiently and effectively to compete in the globalizing economy.

References

Abken, P. 1998. Interest-Rate Caps, Collars, and Floors. *Economic Review* (November–December): 2–21.

Alexander, C. (ed.). 1998. *Risk Management Analysis.* New York: John Wiley & Sons.

Andersen, A. 1995. *Managing Business Risks: An Integrated Approach.* New York: The Economist Intelligence Unit.

Angermueller, H. 1987. The Customer Is Always Right: The Case for Functional Regulation of Financial Services. Federal Reserve Bank of Chicago.

Arayama, Y., and Mourdoukoutas, P. 1999. *China Against Herself: Imitation or Innovation in International Business.* Westport, Conn.: Quorum Books.

———. 2000. *The Rise and Fall of Abacus Banking in Japan and China.* Westport, Conn.: Quorum Books.

Badger, P. 1995. Financial Insurance, Interest Rate Risk, and Derivatives. *The Bankers Magazine* 72 (3): 32–40.

Bank of International Settlements. 1999. *Central Bank Survey of Foreign Exchange Derivatives,* Basle, May.

Benston, G. 1990. *The Separation of Commercial and Investment Banking.* New York: Oxford University Press.

Bernstein, P. 1998. *Against the Gods: The Remarkable Story of Risk.* New York: John Wiley & Sons.

Bhansali, V. 1998. *Pricing and Managing Exotic and Hybrid Options.* Homewood, Ill.: Irwin Library of Investments and Finance.

Bolger A. 1999. Risk Control Becomes Good Business. *Financial Times*, 27 June, p. 3.

Boyd, J. 1997. Banks in International Trade Finance: Transferring the Risks. *Banks in International Trade and Finance* (May–June): 32–35.

Brown, B., and R. C. Geist. 1983. *Financial Futures Markets.* New York: St. Martin's Press.

Cade, E. 1997. *Managing Banking Risks.* London: Woodhead Publishing.

Carter, M. 1995. Risk Management in the Global Arena. *Bank Management* 72 (3): 20–31.

Casserley, D., and C. Wilson. 1994. Demystifying Derivatives. *Bank Management* 70 (3): 40–47.

Cates, D. 1994. Strategic Pathways. *Bank Management* 70 (3): 48–53.

Chance, D. 1998. *An Introduction into Financial Derivatives.* New York: Dryden Press.

Cisco Systems. 1999. *Annual Report.* San Jose, California.

Cohen, Jackie. 1996. Playing the Relationship Trump Card. *Bank Technology News* 9, no. 7: 1.

Cooper, K., and Fraser, D. 1984. *Banking Deregulation and the New Competition in Financial Services.* Cambridge: Ballinger.

Costanzo, C. 1997. Coaxing The Masses with Sticks, Carrots. *Bank Technology News* 10, no. 6: 1.

Crosse, H., and G. Hempel. 1980. *Management Policies for Banks.* 3d ed. Englewood Cliffs, N.J.: Prentice Hall.

Crutchfield, E. Jr. 1994. Spanning Traditional Boundaries. *Bank Management* 70 (5): 51–60.

Cumming, Christine M. 1998. Financial Service Regulation. *Business Economics* 33, no. 4.

D'Amato, A. M. 1995. Derivative Financial Instruments Relating to Banks and Financial Institutions. U.S. Senate Hearing, 5 January, pp. 1–215.

Das, Sattyajit. 1997. *Credit Derivatives: Trading and Management of Credit and Default Risk.* New York: John Wiley and Sons.

Dempster, M. A., and S. Pliska (eds). 1997. *Mathematics of Derivative Securities.* Cambridge: Cambridge University Press.

Eager, R. 1995. The New Federal Interstate Banking And Branching Legislation. *The Bankers Magazine* 71 (6): 23–28.

The Economist. 1999. On a Wing and a Prayer. International Banking Survey, 17 April.

Feldman, R. 1995. Will Securitization Revolution Spread? *Federal Reserve Bank of Minneapolis*, September, 23–30.

Finerty, J. 1998. Russian Settlements Will Put Credit Derivatives to the Test. *American Banker* 163 (December): 12.

Fong, G., and J. Vasicek. 1999. A Multidimensional Framework for Risk Analysis. *Financial Analysts Journal* 55 (1): 13–26.

Furash, E. 1994. Risk Challenges and Opportunities. *Bank Management* 70 (3): 34–44.

The Globecon Group, Ltd. 1995. *Derivatives Engineering: A Guide to Structuring, Pricing, and Marketing Derivatives.* Chicago: Irwin Professional Publishing.

Greenspan, A. 1998. Private-Sector Refinancing of the Needy Fund: Long-Term Capital Management. Congressional testimony, 1 October, p. 2.

Griffin, D. 1995. Due-Diligence Minimizes Credit Risk. *Bank Management* 72 (3): 71–75.

Gup, B. 1984. *Management of Financial Institutions.* Boston: Houghton Mifflin.

Haight, G. T. 1997. An Overview of Risk Management in Banking. *The Bankers Magazine* 180 (3): 10–16.

Haight, G. T., and C. J. Kelly. 1995. The Role of Derivatives as an Asset/Liability Management Tool. *The Bankers Magazine* 180 (3): 22–22.

Haines, W. 1966. *Money, Prices, and Policy.* New York: McGraw-Hill.

Hull, J. 1998. *Introduction to Futures and Options Markets.* 3d ed. Upper Saddle River, N.J.: Prentice Hall.

Indick, M. 1995. Considerations for Interstate Banking Transactions. *The Bankers Magazine* 178 (6): 3–5.

Jorion, P. 1997. *Value at Risk: The New Benchmark for Controlling Derivatives Risk.* New York: McGraw-Hill.

Keller, W. 1995. Investment Products—The New Off-Balance Sheet Risk. *The Bankers Magazine* 178 (2): 35–39.

Kimball, R. 1997. Innovations in Performance: Measurement in Banking. *New England Economic Review* (May–June): 23–38.

Koch, T. 1988. *Bank Management.* New York: Dryden Press.

Kolor, J. 1996. Home Banking Crossroads: The Web, the PC, or Both. *Bank Technology News* 9, no. 9: 1.

Lazonick, W., and M. O'Sullivan. 1997. Finance and Industrial Development: Evolution to Market Control. *Financial History Review* 4: 117–138.

Leland, E. H. 1999. Beyond Mean Variance: Performance Measurement in a Nonsymmetrical World. *Financial Analysts Journal* 55 (1): 27–36.

Maisel, S. (ed.). 1981. *Risk and Capital Adequacy in Commercial Banks.* Chicago: University of Chicago Press.

Managing Risk. 1994. *Business Week*, 31 October, special report, 86–92.

Markowitz, H. 1999. *Portfolio Selection.* 2d ed. Cambridge: Blackwell.

Mason, J. 1979. *Financial Management of Commercial Banks.* Boston: Warren, Gorham & Lamont.

Mayer, M. 1998. *The Bankers: The Next Generation.* New York: Truman Talley Books/Plume.

———. 1999. Risk Reduction in the New Financial Architecture. The Jerome Levy Institute of Bard College, *Public Policy Brief* 56A: 1–2.

McClave, N. 1996. Bank Mandate: Breakthrough Approaches to Managing Risk. *Bank Management* 72 (2): 15–22.

McCrimmon, K., and D. Wehrung. 1986. *Taking Risks: The Management of Uncertainty.* New York: The Free Press.

McLeod, K. 1997. On the Road to "Virtual Banking." *The Bankers Magazine* (July–August): 3–8.

Meadows, R., and N. McClave. 1996. Bank Mandate: Breakthrough Approaches to Managing Risk. *Bank Management* (March–April): 29–35.

Merging Commercial and Investment Banking. 1987. Chicago: Federal Reserve Bank of Chicago.

Michaud, R. O. 1998. *Efficient Asset Management.* Harvard: Business School Press.

Microsoft. 1999. *Annual Report.* Seattle, Washington.

Milken, M. 1999. Prosperity and Social Capital. *The Wall Street Journal,* 23 June, A8.

Minehan, E. C., and K. Simons. 1995. Managing Risk in the 90s: What Should We Be Asking about Derivatives? *New England Economic Review* (September–October): 1–25.

Mourdoukoutas, P. 1999. *The Global Corporation.* Westport, Conn.: Quorum Books

MTIC Technologies. 1999. *Annual Report.* Anaheim, California.

Nolan, F. 1995. Documentation: The Key to Containing Derivatives Risk. *The Bankers Magazine* (May–June): 15–21.

OECD. 1987. *Asset and Liability Management by the Banks.* Paris: OECD.

Park, S. 1994. Explanations of the Increased Riskiness of Banks in the 1980s. *Federal Reserve Bank of St. Louis* (July–August): 1–23.

———. 1998. Credit Risk. *ABA Banking Journal* 90 (August): 30.

Patrikis, E. 1997. Retail Banking Evolution and Risks. *Federal Reserve Bank of New York,* 30 October, pp. 18–25.

Petrou, K. 1997. Risk Management in an Era of Expanded Product Offerings: The New Supervision-by-Risk Framework. *The Banker Magazine* 180 (3): 17–30.

Randle, W. 1995. Delivering the Future: Redefining the Role of Banks in a New Competitive Environment. *Bank Management Review* (January–February): 45–48.

Reed, W. E. 1963. *Commercial Bank Management.* New York: Harper and Row.

Rescher, N. 1983. *Risk: A Philosophical Introduction to the Theory of Risk Evaluation and Management.* Lanham, Md.: University Press of America.

Rose, S. P. 2000. *Money and Capital Markets.* 7th ed. Boston: Irwin–McGraw-Hill.

Saunders, A. 2000. *Financial Institutions Management.* 3d ed. New York: McGraw-Hill.

Schwarz, E. 1979. *How to Use Interest Rate Futures Contracts.* Homewood, Ill.: Dow Jones–Irwin.

Seiberg, J. 1997. Credit Derivatives Added to Market Risk Rules. *American Banker* 162 (June): 4.

Simons, K. 1995. Interest Rate Derivatives and Asset–Liability Management by Commercial Banks. *New England Economic Review* (January–February): 17–28.

Simons, R. 1999. How Risky Is Your Company? *Harvard Business Review* (May–June): 85–95.

Smith, B. 1994. Re-Inventing Investment Management. *Bank Management* 177 (3): 60–64.

Smithson, W. 1998. *Managing Financial Risks: A Guide to Derivative Products, Financial Engineering, and Value Maximization.* 3d ed. New York: McGraw-Hill.

Southern Company. 1999. *Annual Report.* Atlanta, Georgia.

Steinherr, A. 1998. *Derivatives: The Wild Beast of Finance.* Chichester, U.K.: Wiley.

Stigum, M., and R. Branch, Jr. 1983. *Managing Bank Assets and Liabilities.* Homewood, Ill.: Dow Jones–Irwin.

Stock Sales Cut into Cross-Holdings. 1998. *The Nikkei Weekly*, 11 January, editorial, p. 11.

Strategic Financial Risk Management. 1993. London: The Economist Intelligence Unit.

Svare, C. 1998. The Information Technology Challenge: Orchestrating the Bottom Line. *Banking Strategies* 74 (1): 50–56.

Suzuki, Y. (ed.). 1997. *Money and Banking in Contemporary Japan.* Oxford: Claredon Press.

Taylor, F. 1996. *Mastering Derivative Markets.* London: FT Pitman.

Teweles, J. R., and F. J. Jones. 1998. *Who Wins, Who Loses, and Why.* 3d ed. New York: McGraw-Hill.

Treacy, F. W., and S. M. Carey. 1998. Credit Risk Rating at Large U.S. Banks. *Federal Reserve Bulletin* 84 (11): 1–27.

Twrenbaum, R. 1995. Investment Management: Fulfilling the Promise. *Bank Management Review* (May–June): 49–53.

Waldrop, R. 1999. Financial Services. In *US Industry and Trade Outlook '99.* New York: McGraw-Hill.

Wilmot, P., and S. Howson. 1995. *The Mathematics of Financial Derivatives.* Boston: Cambridge University Press.

Index

Absolute advantage, 126–129
Aggregate risk measures, 43
Amendment of the Banking
    Holding Act, 54
Asset and liability management,
    60–61
Asset swaps, 106–107

Bank Holding Company Act, 54
Banking Act of 1935, 54
Banking Merger Act of 1960, 54
Banking risk classifications,
    15–16, 159–161
Banking risk identification, 16–18,
    159–161
Basle Accord, 55, 66
Basle Committee, 66–67
Bear call spread, 89
Bear put spread, 90–91
"Big Bang," 67–68
Bull call spread, 89
Bull put spread, 90

Butterfly call spread, 90

Caps, 91
Chicago Board of Trade (CBOT),
    75–77
Collars, 92
Commercial loan theory, 60–61
Commodity price risk, 16, 21
Consumer Protection/Transpar-
    ency Acts, 55
Conversion foreign exchange risk,
    20–21
Convexity, 23, 34
Counterparty risk, 106–107
Credit derivatives, 104–105
Credit options, 104, 158
Credit risk, 16–17, 26, 28, 104–
    105, 158–159
Credit risk management, 62–63,
    97, 158–159
Credit swaps, 105–106
Cumulative gap, 36–37

Currency swap, 6, 152

Depository Institutions Deregulation and Monetary Act of 1980, 65
Directive 89/647, 66
Discount/premium bid rate, 142
Douglas Amendment, 54
Duration analysis, 23, 28–30

"Escorted Convoy System," 67–68
Eurodollar interest rate futures, 119–121
European Union directives, 66–67
Evolution of banking risks, 51–53
Exercise and settlement, 81

Financial derivatives, 6, 7, 73
Financial derivatives risk, 16, 21
Financial derivatives value, 7
Financial intermediation, 1, 58–59
Floors, 92
Foreign currency futures, 71–72, 144, 157–159
Foreign currency swap, 151, 154, 160–161
Foreign exchange risk, 16, 20, 37–39, 75, 135, 160–161
Forward discount, 142
Forward foreign currency contracts, 75 136–137, 157
Forward premium, 142
Forward rate agreements, 73, 113–114, 157–158
Forwards, 74–75
Futures contract margins, 77
Futures contracts, 75–76
Futures hedging versus speculation, 76–77
FX futures, 145
FX sensitivity analysis, 23, 38–39

Garn–St. Germain Act of 1982, 65
Glass–Steagall Act, 54
Globalization, 50–53, 70–71
Global positions in OTC foreign exchange derivative contracts, 137

Government deregulation, 46, 156
Gramm and Leach Act of 1999, 65

Hedging a short FX position, 138

Income risk, 16,18, 33–37
Interest rate cap, 123, 157
Interest rate collar, 126
Interest rate floor, 109
Interest rate futures, 73, 113, 116, 157–158
Interest rate gaps, 111–113, 124
Interest rate options, 119–120
Interest rate risk management, 16, 108
Interest rate spread, 128
International Banking Act of 1978, 55, 56
Investment portfolio risks, 16, 21, 39–42

Legal risk, 16–17
Liability swaps, 124–126
Liquidation risk, 16, 21
Liquidity risk, 16, 23–26
Liquidity risk management, 58–59
London International Financial Exchange (LIFE), 75

Macaulay's formula, 29
Management methods, 11, 45–46, 51–52, 113, 159–160
Margin requirements, 76
Market risks, 18–21
Marking-to-market, 146
Markowitz, H., 39–40, 41
Maturity ladder, 25
McFadden Act, 54
Mean value optimization, 41–42
Modified duration, 31–33
Multinationalization, 50, 53

National Currency Act of 1863, 54
Negative interest rate gap, 111
New York Mercantile Exchange, 76
New York State Insurance Legislation, 54
Nontraditional banking risks, 157

Operation risk, 16
Option contracts, 6, 78–79
Options buyers, 78–80
Options contracts classification, 79–81, 157
Options hedging versus speculation, 87–88
Options markets, 85–86
Options premium, 82–84
Options rewards, 87
Options risks, 87
Options sellers 78–80

Payer's swaption, 122
Plain vanilla swaps, 125–128
Political risk, 16–17
Portfolio diversification, 41–42
Portfolio volatility, 42
Position risk, 16, 18, 28–33
Positive interest rate gap, 111

Ratio analysis, 26–28
Receiver's swaption, 122
Regulation Z, 55
Relationship banking, 3, 5, 72
Relative gap, 37–38
Riegle–Neal Interstate Banking and Branching Efficiency Act of 1994, 65
Risk attitudes, 14
Risk management, 1, 5, 8, 11, 12, 45–46, 51–52, 71, 73, 112
Risk management methods, 73
Risk management tools, 71
Risk monitoring and control, 45–49
Risk versus return, 41
Russian debt moratorium, 69

Scoring and asset classification, 101–104
Scoring and ranking, 98–103, 159–160
Secutirization, 61–62
Selective FX futures, 145
Selective interest rate futures, 117
Selective interest rate options, 121
Simple and modified duration, 32
Simple duration, 32
Single and aggregate risk measures, 23
Single risk measures, 22–23
Spot rate, 142
Spread, 89
Straddle, 89
Straddle holder, 150
Strike price, 81
Swaps, 6, 91, 159–161
Swaptions, 92

Time value of an option's contract, 86–87
Total risk management, 43, 44, 45
Traditional banking risks, 157
Transaction or net income foreign exchange risk, 20

Underlying interest, 80–81
U.S. banking regulations, 54–55
U.S. financial deregulation, 65–66, 156
U.S. Treasury futures options, 131

Value at risk, 6, 23, 44–45
Variance and beta, 39–42

WTO, 63–66

ABOUT THE AUTHORS

Panos Angelopoulos is a Credit Analyst at Alpha Bank and has worked as a consultant to the Ministry of Education on the development of courses in banking and stock markets, both in Greece. He teaches in colleges and continuing education programs and holds an M.A. in economics from the City University of New York. Previously he worked in the Risk Management Department and the Credit Policy Department of the Ionian Bank and at the Center of Economic Planning and Research, also in Greece.

Panos Mourdoukoutas is Professor of Economics, Long Island University, New York. He has traveled extensively throughout Europe and Asia as an adviser to government and business organizations, with extended stays at Nagoya University, Japan. Among his many publications are four books from Quorum: *The Global Corporation* and *Collective Entrepreneurship in a Globalizing Economy* (both 1999), and with (Yuko Arayama) *The Rise and Fall of Abacus Banking in Japan and China* (2000) and *China Against Herself* (1999).